MW01620711

PEOPLE OF DESTINY

Millenial Press, Inc.
11968 South Doves Landing Drive
Riverton, Utah 84065

Publisher's Cataloging-in-Publication Data
(Provided by Quality Books, Inc.)

Dean L. Larsen
People of Destiny: The Special Role of God's Covenant Children
by Dean L. Larsen – 1st ed.
p. cm.
Includes index.

ISBN 0-9660231-9-6

PEOPLE OF DESTINY

Dean L. Larsen

Millennial Press
Salt Lake City, Utah

Table of Contents

People of Destiny
The Special Role of God's Covenant Children

Introduction

In the days of Enoch, the people of the earth were ripening in iniquity. The voice of the Lord came to Enoch, saying: "I am angry with this people, and my fierce anger is kindled against them; for their hearts have waxed hard, and their ears are dull of hearing, and their eyes cannot see afar off" (Moses 6:26).

When people lose sight of the Lord's purposes, their interests, concerns, and objectives in life tend to focus upon the tangible things of the world. The acquisition of these things and the pleasures that are derived from them become the consuming motivation of their lives. They tend not to reflect much on historical precedents, and living for the here and now obscures vision of portending events.

We are living in a time when the conditions of the world are much as they were in the days of Enoch. The Lord has warned us that the world is ripening again in iniquity (see D&C 18:6; 29:9). As we draw nearer to the time when the Savior will return in glory to usher in His millennial reign, it is vitally important for Latter-day Saints to have a clear view of their historical roots as a covenant people of the Lord. They must also be able to see clearly the role that they will yet play as the great day of the Lord approaches. In this sense, their eyes must be able to see afar off. The vision of their covenant status cannot be obscured by the enticements of a materialistic, short-sighted world.

Mormon's fervent, final injunction to his own people and to those who would be associated with them in the last days was "Know ye that ye are of the house of Israel" (Mormon 7:2). What does it mean to be of the house of Israel? Why is it important to be of this special heritage? Who were those in ancient times that were included under this mantle? What has happened to them? Where are they and their posterity today? What does the Lord expect of them still?

These questions have remained with me over the years. As I have studied the scriptures and pondered the instructions of latter-day prophets, I feel I have found some of the answers. There is much yet to be learned as the fascinating story of these covenant people continues to unfold. The most dramatic, exciting events in the history of this earth are still ahead of us, and the people of Israel will be the principal actors in these culminating scenes that will precede the Lord's glorious return.

A feeling that others may share my intense interest in the house of Israel has prompted me to record the observations that comprise the chapters which follow. It should be understood by the reader that much of the content will reflect my own thinking and conclusions about all that the Lord has revealed concerning Israel. I make no claim to new or revelatory information. I have simply attempted to draw upon the numerous references scattered among the scriptures and the declarations of modern prophets to tell the story of a special people. That story is still unfolding. The final chapters are bound to be the most dramatic and compelling of all.

Part I

God's Purpose in Establishing A Chosen People

CHAPTER 1

Why A Chosen People?

It seems reasonable to ask the question: Why would the Lord choose a certain group of people to honor and favor in particular ways? Does this not seem to contradict his declaration that he is no respecter of persons (D&C 1:35)? Does not God's love extend equitably to all of his children? Is it his intent to exalt one group of people above another?

Part of the answer to these related questions may well have begun during a premortal time over which a veil has been drawn. We know from what the Lord revealed to Abraham that all those who kept their "first estate" and chose to enter mortal life would be "added upon" (Abraham 3:26). The divine plan of progress included a provision for a mortal experience and was intended to offer rich opportunities for growth and advancement to all who became participants. The ultimate prospect for those who entered into this experience was to have "glory added upon their heads forever and ever" (Abraham 3:26). Much of the detail of what preparation may have been necessary in that period referred to as the "first estate" is obscured by the veil that has been drawn over our recollection of that time. Only fragmentary glimpses have been provided in the Lord's revelations. Abraham was allowed a brief view into the premortal period and recorded the following: "Now the Lord had shown unto me, Abraham, the intelligences that were organized before the world was; and among all these there were many of the noble and great ones;

"And God saw these souls that they were good, and he stood in the midst of them, and he said: These I will make my rulers: for he stood among those that were spirits, and he saw that they were good: and he said unto me: Abraham, thou art one of them: thou wast chosen before thou wast born" (Abraham 3:22-23).

Many interesting implications can be drawn from Abraham's disclosure regarding the premortal state. It appears that in the premortal experiences of those spirits whom Abraham saw, some had developed and proved themselves beyond their fellow spirits. They had demonstrated a capacity to carry special responsibilities when they entered the "second estate," or mortal life. Among these was Abraham, who was "chosen" before he was born. Chosen for what? He was to be a "ruler" or a leader during his mortal experience. It appears he was qualified to exert a positive influence upon his peers who would join him in this new adventure in mortal life. His being "chosen" was more than a special honor that he had earned. It was the conferring of a sobering charge and responsibility.

Others were given a disclosure similar to that received by Abraham. Jeremiah, another Old Testament prophet, recorded: "Then the word of the Lord came unto me, saying, Before I formed thee in the belly I knew thee; and before thou camest forth out of the womb I sanctified thee, and I ordained thee a prophet unto the nations" (Jeremiah 1:4-5).

It seems reasonable to conclude from these scriptural reflections that certain spirits had prepared themselves in premortal life to carry out particular responsibilities when coming into mortality. They were those whom the Lord felt he could trust with the charge to be a sustaining and guiding influence for their fellow spirits in the challenging and testing experiences of mortal life.

If there is a degree of validity to this contention, then it is not difficult to understand why the Lord would be so distressed when these trusted, "chosen" spirits would at times turn aside from their responsibility in mortality, reject their God, and become a negative force to lead others astray.

In his book The Covenant People, W. J. Cameron defines the purpose and mission of a chosen people. He writes:

"A man will rise and demand, 'By what right does God choose one race of people above another?' I like that form of the question. It is much better than asking by what right God degrades one people beneath another, although that is implied. God's grading is always upward. If he raises up a nation, it is that other nations may be raised up through its ministry. If he exalts a great man, an apostle of liberty, or science, or faith, it is that he might raise a degraded people to a better condition. The Divine selection is not a prize, a compliment paid to the man or the race - it is a burden imposed. To appoint a chosen people is not a pandering to the racial vanity of a 'superior people'; it is a yoke bound upon the necks of those who are chosen for a special purpose" (The Covenant People, Destiny Publishers, Merrimac, Massachusetts, 1966, pg. 8).

In his early life Abraham lived in the land of the Chaldeans. His father and his people had turned to the worship of the gods of the Chaldeans. Stirred by the intimations of his foreordained responsibility, Abraham sought for the knowledge and the right to fulfill his role as a ruler and a leader while he passed through his mortal estate. Abraham said: "Behold, I lifted up my voice unto the Lord my God, and the Lord hearkened and heard..."

"And his voice was unto me: Abraham, Abraham, behold, my name is Jehovah, and I have heard thee."

"Behold I will lead thee by my hand, and I will take thee, to put upon thee my name, even the Priesthood of thy father, and my power shall be over thee.

"As it was with Noah so shall it be with thee; but through thy ministry my name shall be known in the earth forever, for I am thy God" (Abraham 1:15, 16, 18, 19).

As Abraham demonstrated his willingness to obey the Lord and accept his foreordained responsibility, the Lord expanded the promise and covenant that he had initiated earlier with Abraham. It is in this additional unfolding of the covenant that the role of Abraham and his righteous descendants is made manifest.

"And I will make of thee a great nation," the Lord promised, "And I will bless thee above measure, and make thy name great among all the nations, and thou shalt be a blessing unto thy seed after thee, that in their hands they shall bear this ministry and priesthood unto all nations" (Abraham 2:9).

Here in this covenant statement is a very significant disclosure. Abraham and his righteous seed are to be the instruments the Lord will use to "bear this ministry and priesthood unto all nations." They are to become the Lord's agent people to further his work and his purposes among all of the spirits who enter mortal life. This was the honor and distinction conferred upon Abraham and his posterity through the Lord's covenant. This was the burden of responsibility bound upon their necks for all generations to come.

"In thee," the Lord declared, "shall all the families of the earth be blessed" (Genesis 12:3). It was an awesome charge to those who had been chosen in the world of spirits to take upon them this covenant.

The Apostle Peter revealed his knowledge of this special responsibility when he said to the Jews: "Ye are the children of the prophets, and of the covenant that God made with our fathers, saying unto Abraham, And in thy seed shall all the kindreds of the earth be blessed" (Acts 3:25). Moses, in his final instructions to the people whom he had led through the wilderness for forty years, reminded them: "For thou art an holy people unto the Lord thy God: the Lord thy God hath chosen thee to be a special people unto himself, above all the people that are upon the face of the earth" (Deuteronomy 7:6).

"And the Lord hath avouched thee this day to be his peculiar people..." (Deuteronomy 26:18).

Through the prophet Isaiah the Lord confirmed this charge to those who had become heirs of the covenant made to Abraham. "Ye are my witnesses, saith the Lord, and my servants whom I have chosen..." (Isaiah 43:10).

"...I will also give thee for a light to the Gentiles, that thou mayest be my salvation unto the ends of the earth" (Isaiah 49:6).

In the scriptural references that have been cited, at least a partial answer to the question propounded in this chapter seems to emerge. Why, indeed, a chosen people? To be identified with this special group obviously carries some honor and distinction that appear to bear implications of qualifications demonstrated in an earlier sphere of existence. But above all else is the clear manifestation of the special responsibility placed upon those of the covenant to be the Lord's agent people, his instruments for offering the blessings of salvation to all of God's children who enter the second estate. It is, indeed, a heavy burden that some generations of the covenant people have set aside in order to follow their own selfish and indolent whims, as succeeding chapters will disclose. It is a trust that God has laid upon those in whom he has placed his confidence. As they respond to this trust, they make certain their own exaltation and eternal life as the Lord has promised. And they become his cohorts in facilitating the achievement of immortality and eternal life for all of God's children.

CHAPTER 2

What Does it Mean to Be A Covenant People?

The dictionary gives as one definition of "covenant" "the conditional promises made to man by God as revealed in the Scripture." (The Random House College Dictionary, Revised Edition, 1980). This definition implies that the promises made by God in his covenants are predicated upon compliance to terms which are set by him. Man does not negotiate the terms. He becomes a party to the covenant by agreeing to comply with God's requirements and thereby qualifies as a recipient of the promises which God has extended.

There are specific individual covenants into which one may enter. Generally these are associated with ordinances which, in some cases, require an outward performance or action symbolic of some aspect of the covenant, as in the case of baptism and the sacrament of the Lord's supper. These are essential for one's individual spiritual development and progress toward greater perfection.

It appears that God's covenant with Israel as a people has some distinctive elements. These can be discovered in part by a careful review of the promises and conditions outlined by the Lord, as the covenant pronouncements have been made and recorded in the scriptures. Compliance with the individual covenants may be essential to one's qualifying for participation in the more all-inclusive covenant made with the house of Israel as a people. Some of the particular elements in God's covenant with the house of Israel include:

1. They will become a great nation whose name will be great among all nations (Abr. 2:9).
2. They will be the Lord's agents for taking the gospel and the priesthood to all nations (Abr. 2:9).
3. They will become a blessing to all the families of the earth by their physical presence as the literal seed of Abraham and his posterity with whom the covenant is renewed (Abr. 2:11) (Gen. 22:18).
4. Those who bless and uphold Israel will be blessed (Abr. 2:11).
5. Those who curse Israel will be cursed (Abr. 2:11).
6. Israel will be given lands upon the earth as an everlasting inheritance (Gen. 17:8), (Gen. 26:4), (Gen. 28:3, 4-13), (1 Nephi 14:2), (3 Nephi 21:22), (Ether 13:6, 8, 10, 11), (1 Nephi 22:12).
7. All who accept the gospel of Jesus Christ and accept him as their Savior will be joined with the house of Israel and become part of the covenant people (Abr. 2:10), (1 Nephi 14:2), (2 Nephi 30:2), (3 Nephi 16:13), (3 Nephi 21:22).

A comment on each of these facets to the covenant God made with Israel may be useful.

1. Israel Will Become A Great Nation

This promise does not pertain exclusively to Old Testament times, although even in that period the people of Israel had become a great nation–a force to be reckoned with in a political sense. Abraham was promised that his posterity would become as numerous as the stars of heaven and the sands upon the seashore (Gen. 22:17), (Abr. 3:13, 14).

Isaiah as well as Nephi looked ahead to a time in the latter days when many of the children of the covenant people who had lost their identity would be brought to a remembrance of their heritage. "The children which thou shalt have, after thou hast lost the other, shall say again in thine ears, The place is too strait for me: give place to me that I may dwell.

"Then thou shalt say in thine heart, who hath begotten me these, seeing I have lost my children, and am desolate, a captive, and removing to and fro? and who hath brought up these? Behold, I was left alone; these, where have they been" (Isaiah 49:20, 21), (1 Nephi 21:20, 21)?

As the Lord mentions the latter-day return of the lost tribes, he speaks of the "boundaries of the everlasting hills" trembling at their presence (D&C 133:31).

As conditions among the nations of the earth deteriorate and anarchy begins to prevail, the Lord's faithful covenant people will manifest a power that will act as a deterrent to any who may feel enmity toward them or who may have designs upon their possessions. "And it shall be said among the wicked; Let us not go up to battle against Zion, for the inhabitants of Zion are terrible; wherefore, we cannot stand" (D&C 45:70).

This is reflected further in the Lord's prophetic words concerning Israel in the Zion that will be established in the last days: "And, now, behold, if Zion do these things she shall prosper, and spread herself, and become very glorious, very great, and very terrible.

"And the nations of the earth shall honor her, and shall say: Surely, Zion is the city of our God, and surely Zion cannot fail, neither be moved out of her place, for God is there, and the hand of the Lord is there..." (D&C 97:18-19).

2. Israel To Be The Lord's Agent People.

(This aspect of the covenant has been dealt with in some measure in the preceding chapter.)

It is apparent that the Lord expects his covenant people to live so much in accordance with the principles of the gospel that they will be a model for others to follow, a motivation to those who observe the blessings flowing to an obedient people, and in this find an incentive to do likewise. Isaiah prophesied of this important role that Israel would carry. "For, behold, darkness shall cover the earth, and gross darkness the people: but the Lord shall arise upon thee, and his glory shall be seen upon thee.

"And the Gentiles shall come to thy light, and kings to the brightness of thy rising" (Isaiah 60:2, 3).

"And their seed shall be known among the Gentiles, and their offspring among the people: and all that see them shall acknowledge them, that they are the seed which the Lord hath blessed" (Isaiah 61:9).

What a tremendous responsibility is placed upon the people of Israel to be a model of righteousness! What a blessing to be endowed with such a trust! But the Lord makes it clear that to be of the chosen lineage alone is not sufficient. Obedience to God's laws is the fundamental requirement. This is why he would inspire the Book of Mormon prophet, Nephi, to admonish: "And now my beloved brethren...I, Nephi, would not suffer that ye should suppose that ye are more righteous than the Gentiles shall be. For, behold, except ye shall keep the commandments of God ye shall all likewise perish....

"For behold, I say unto you that as many of the Gentiles as will repent are the covenant people of the Lord; and as many of the Jews as will not repent shall be cast off...." (2 Nephi 30:1, 2).

Marvelous blessings are in store for the obedient of the house of Israel, but they are not intended only for the literal seed. As others, not of the chosen lineage, respond to the righteous example of the covenant people and align themselves with principles of truth, they also enter into the covenant and enjoy all of the promises to Abraham: "..For as many as receive this Gospel shall be called after thy name, and shall be accounted thy seed, and shall rise up and bless thee, as their father" (Abr. 2:10).

3. Israel, As Abraham's Literal Seed, To Become A Blessing To All Nations And All The Families Of The Earth.

This does not suggest that the day will come when all of the inhabitants of the earth will bear some of the blood of Abraham. It does seem to point to a time, however, when those who are of the blood of Abraham, Isaac, and Jacob will be sufficiently dispersed among the nations of the earth that they will be in a position, by virtue of their location, to exert a blessed influence among their neighbors and their peers. The Lord promised Abraham that "...in thy seed after thee (that is to say, the literal seed of the body) shall all the families of the earth be blessed, even with the blessings of the Gospel..." (Abr. 2:11).

4. Those Who Bless And Uphold Israel Will Be Blessed.

In speaking through his prophets concerning the latter-day gathering and restoration of Israel, the Lord makes it clear that there will be those among the nations of the earth who will give assistance to this great effort. Their part in this work will result in blessings for them. Nephi quoted from the prophetic words of Isaiah when he wrote:

"Thus saith the Lord God: Behold, I will lift up mine hand to the Gentiles, and set up my standard to the people; and they shall bring thy sons in their arms, and thy daughters shall be carried upon their shoulders.

"And kings shall be thy nursing fathers, and their queens thy nursing mothers; they shall bow down to thee with their face towards the earth, and lick up the dust of thy feet; and thou shalt know that I am the Lord; for they shall not be ashamed that wait for me" (1 Nephi 21:22, 23).

"...the time cometh that after all the house of Israel have been scattered and confounded, that the Lord God will raise up a mighty nation among the Gentiles..., and by them shall our seed be scattered,

"And after our seed is scattered the Lord God will proceed to do a marvelous work among the Gentiles which shall be of great worth to our seed; wherefore it is likened unto their being nourished by the Gentiles and being carried in their arms and upon their shoulders.

"And it shall also be of great worth unto the Gentiles... (1 Nephi 22:7-9).

Nephi spoke in his own words concerning the benefits that would come to the Gentiles in the Americas who would recognize the Lord's hand and align themselves with this great latter-day effort. He promised, "And it shall come to pass, that if the Gentiles shall hearken unto the Lamb of God in that day that he shall manifest himself unto them in word, and also in power, in very deed, unto the taking away of their stumbling blocks –

"And harden not their hearts against the Lamb of God, they shall be numbered among the seed of thy father; yea, they shall be numbered among the house of Israel; and they shall be a blessed people upon the promised land forever..." (1 Nephi 14:1, 2).

5. Those Who Curse Israel Will Be Cursed.

The Lord gives a solemn warning to those who curse the house of Israel and raise an opposition to the fulfillment of the Lord's promises to his covenant people.

"...Ye need not any longer hiss, nor spurn, nor make game of the Jews, nor any of the remnant of the house of Israel; for behold, the Lord remembereth his covenant unto them, and he will do unto them according to that which he hath sworn.

"Therefore ye need not suppose that ye can turn the right hand of the Lord unto the left, that he may not execute judgment unto the fulfilling of the covenant which he hath made unto the house of Israel" (3 Nephi 29:8, 9).

Through Nephi and Isaiah the Lord gives this dire warning to those who oppose Israel: "...I will contend with him that contendeth with thee, and I will save thy children.

"And I will feed them that oppress thee with their own flesh; and they shall be drunken with their own blood as with sweet wine; and all flesh shall know that I am thy Savior and thy Redeemer, the Mighty One of Jacob" (1 Nephi 21: 25, 26) (Isaiah 49:25, 26).

The Lord also declared, "Behold, they shall surely gather together against thee, not by me; whosoever shall gather together against thee shall fall for thy sake."

"No weapon that is formed against thee shall prosper; and every tongue that shall revile against thee in judgment thou shalt condemn..." (3 Nephi 22:15, 17).

6. Israel Will Be Given Lands as an Everlasting Inheritance.

A key element in the Lord's covenant with Israel is that they will receive as a lasting inheritance specific lands upon the earth for the benefit of their posterity. The Lord promised Abraham: "And I will give unto thee, and to thy seed after thee, the land wherein thou art a stranger, all the land of Canaan, for an everlasting possession..." (Gen. 17:8).

The promise was repeated to Isaac, Abraham's son, with whom the Lord renewed the covenant: "And I will make thy seed to multiply as the stars of the heaven, and will give unto thy seed all these countries; and in thy seed shall all the nations of the earth be blessed" (Gen. 26:4).

To Jacob, Isaac's son, the same promise and covenant were confirmed: "And God Almighty bless thee, and make thee fruitful, and multiply thee, that thou mayest be a multitude of people;

"And give thee the blessing of Abraham, to thee and to thy seed with thee; that thou mayest inherit the land wherein thou art a stranger, which God gave to Abraham" (Gen. 28:3, 4).

When Lehi came to the Americas with his family and companions, the Lord made similar promises to him and his posterity concerning the new world. Speaking to those who had survived the great destruction in the land at the time of his brief ministry among them, the Savior alluded to those who would in the last days accept his gospel in the same land: "...I will establish my church among them, and they shall come in unto the covenant, and be numbered among this the remnant of Jacob, unto whom I have given this land for their inheritance" (3 Nephi 21:22).

As a confirmation of this promise, the Lord spoke to the prophet Joseph Smith concerning those who would become faithful members of the Church in the last days: "And I hold forth and deign to give unto you greater riches, even a land of promise, a land flowing with milk and honey, upon which there shall be no curse when the Lord cometh;

"And I will give it unto you for the land of your inheritance, if you seek it with all your hearts.

"And this shall be my covenant with you, ye shall have the land for your inheritance, and for the inheritance of your children forever, while the earth shall stand, and ye shall possess it again in eternity, no more to pass away" (D&C 38:18-20).

Nephi pointed to this same element in the covenant God had made to Israel, when speaking of their latter-day restoration and gathering together: "Wherefore, the Lord will proceed to make bare his arm in the eyes of all nations, in bringing about his covenants and his gospel unto those who are of the house of Israel.

"Wherefore, he will bring them again out of captivity, and they shall be gathered to the lands of their inheritance..." (1 Nephi 22:11, 12).

The Book of Mormon prophet, Jacob, recorded the words of the Lord to his own people: "Wherefore, I will consecrate this land unto thy seed, and them who will be numbered among thy seed, forever, for the land of their inheritance..." (2 Nephi 10:19).

As Moroni translated and abridged the records of the Jaredite people in the Book of Mormon, he was impressed to comment on the prophecies of Ether, the Jaredite prophet, concerning the land inheritances that were promised to the house of Israel as part of the covenant. His comments are enlightening: "Wherefore, the remnant of the house of Joseph shall be built upon this land [the Americas]; and it shall be a land of their inheritance; and they shall build up a holy city unto the Lord, like unto the Jerusalem of old; and they shall no more be confounded until the end come and the earth shall pass away" (Ether 13:8).

"And then also cometh the Jerusalem of old; and the inhabitants thereof, blessed are they, for they have been washed in the blood of the Lamb; and they are they who were scattered and gathered in from the four quarters of the earth, and from the north countries, and are partakers of the fulfilling of the covenant which God made with their father, Abraham" (Ether 13:11).

Much of the fulfillment of this great part of the covenant awaits future developments. But the Lord's promise is sure.

7. All who accept Jesus Christ as their Savior and adhere to the principles of the gospel become part of the covenant people.

Many scriptural references already cited support this part of the covenant that God made with his chosen people. Reference has already been made to Nephi's declaration "...as many of the Gentiles as will repent are the covenant people of the Lord..." (2 Nephi 30:2).

The Savior himself declared to the Nephites: "But if the Gentiles will repent and return unto me, saith the Father, behold they shall be numbered among my people, O house of Israel" (3 Nephi 16:13).

He added, still with reference to the Gentiles: "But if they will repent and hearken unto my words, and harden not their hearts, I will establish my Church among them, and they shall come into the covenant and be numbered among this the remnant of Jacob..." (3 Nephi 21:22).

Jacob, the brother of Nephi, spoke of a time when a Gentile nation that would be established in the Americas would be an affliction to the posterity of Lehi and his associates who would be preserved in the land: "...thus saith our God: I will afflict thy seed by the hand of the Gentiles; nevertheless, I will soften the hearts of the Gentiles, that they shall be like a father to them; wherefore, the Gentiles shall be blessed and numbered among the house of Israel" (2 Nephi 10:18).

Part II

Israel in Ancient Times

CHAPTER 3

The Foundations of Ancient Israel

As has been noted, Abraham was promised that the covenant made by God with him would be transmitted to later generations through his seed. It must be understood, however, that the covenant was not renewed through all of Abraham's children. This brings us to the interesting account of Isaac and Ishmael, Abraham's sons.

The reader will recall that Abraham's wife, Saria, went childless into her old age. Because of her barrenness, Saria asked Abraham to take her handmaiden, an Egyptian woman named Hagar, as a second wife so that Abraham could have children. Abraham hearkened unto Saria, and from his union with Hagar, a son was conceived.

Hagar apparently flaunted her fertility before Saria, and a great animosity developed between the two. Hagar was driven from the household and fled into the wilderness. An angel of the Lord appeared to Hagar and told her to humble herself and return to her mistress. The angel advised Hagar that she would give birth to a son who would be called Ishmael. She was promised that she would have numerous posterity. Ishmael would be a "wild man" who would be of a contentious nature: "His hand will be against every man" (Gen. 16:12). Nothing was mentioned with regard to Ishmael's receiving the covenant that God had earlier made with Abraham.

As time passed, the Lord informed Abraham that he would have a son by Saria, his now aged wife. From that time, Saria would be known as Sarah. Abraham was incredulous about the disclosure that Sarah was to become a mother. She was ninety years old. Sarah's incredulity was greater than her husband's. But the Lord's promise was fulfilled, and Isaac was born to Sarah.

Abraham felt compassion for his son Ishmael and made an appeal for him to the Lord: "O that Ishmael might live before thee!" (Genesis 17:18).

The Lord responded to Abraham's appeal with the following:

"And God said, Sarah, thy wife shall bear thee a son indeed; and thou shalt call his name Isaac: and I will establish my covenant with him for an everlasting covenant, and with his seed after him.

"And as for Ishmael, I have heard thee: Behold, I have blessed him, and will make him fruitful, and will multiply him exceedingly, twelve princes will he beget, and I will make him a great nation.

"But my covenant will I establish with Isaac, which Sarah shall bear unto thee at this set time in the next year" (Gen. 17:19-21).

Following Sarah's death, Abraham married again, and took Keturah as a wife. She bore six sons, Zimran, Jokshan, Medan, Midian, Ishbak, and Shuah, all of whom had posterity (Gen. 25:1-4). The account in Genesis records: "And Abraham gave all that he had to Isaac.

"But unto the sons of the concubines, which Abraham had, Abraham gave gifts, and sent them away from Isaac his son, while he yet lived, eastward, unto the east country" (Gen. 25:5, 6).

Only Isaac, of all the sons of Abraham, received the covenant that God had made with his father. This covenant was later confirmed with Isaac by the Lord when he said: "...I will be with thee; for unto thee, and unto thy seed, will I give all these countries, and I will perform the oath which I sware unto Abraham thy father.

"And I will make thy seed to multiply as the stars of heaven, and will given unto thy seed all these countries; and in thy seed shall all the nations of the earth be blessed" (Gen. 26:3, 4).

Abraham made provision for Isaac to marry a wife from among his own people. The accomplishment of this important step is a most interesting story by itself. It is sufficient for the purpose of this narrative, however, to point out that Rebekah, the daughter of Bethuel, was the one who was espoused to become Isaac's bride, and she accepted this arrangement as the will of the Lord.

For a time following her marriage to Isaac, Rebekah remained barren. After earnest prayers on the part of Isaac, and certainly in response to Rebekah's pleas as well, Rebekah conceived. Sensing that the condition of her pregnancy was somewhat unusual, Rebekah went to the Lord for assurance: "Why am I thus?" she asked. "And the Lord said unto her, two nations are in thy womb, and two manner of people shall be separated from thy bowels; and the one people shall be stronger than the other people; and the elder shall serve the younger" (Gen. 25:22, 23).

In this manner, Rebekah learned that she would give birth to twins, and that the two children would be of divergent natures and would follow divergent paths. Of special significance was the disclosure that the first-born of the two children would serve his younger brother. This was altogether contrary to the custom and tradition of the time, and Rebekah carefully tucked away this important revelation in a corner of her mind where it would not be forgotten.

The first of the twins to be born was named Esau. He was described as being red all over and resembled a hairy garment. His brother was called Jacob.

As the two boys grew to maturity, Esau became a cunning hunter and a man of the field. He was Isaac's favorite, and often provided venison for his father's table, which Isaac relished.

Jacob, the record tells us, was a plain man, dwelling in tents. He stayed closer to home and was very much loved by his mother.

In accordance with the tradition of the time, Esau was in line to receive the birthright and to follow in the leadership role of his father. It appears that this sobering responsibility was taken very lightly by Esau. On one occasion, Esau had returned from a long hunt, exhausted and with a consuming appetite. Jacob, it seems, had anticipated this circumstance, and he had made a savory batch of red pottage. Probably with some prodding and encouragement from his mother, Jacob made a proposition to his famished brother. Esau could have the red pottage that he coveted if he would give Jacob, in exchange, his claim to the birthright. Esau's response disclosed his light regard for his distinctive status as the birthright son:

"And Esau said, Behold I am at the point to die: and what profit shall this birthright do to me?

"And Jacob said, Swear to me this day; and he sware unto him: and he sold his birthright to Jacob" (Gen. 25:32, 33).

As Isaac grew old, some of his faculties began to fail him. His eyesight grew dim. Sensing that his days were growing short, he felt the need to pronounce a special blessing upon his eldest, favored son. It can almost be concluded, from the record of the events which followed, that Isaac was unaware of the transaction that had occurred between Esau and Jacob concerning the birthright. Isaac requested that Esau go into the field and secure venison to make a savory meal. On this special occasion, Isaac declared he would give to Esau the formal blessing as the birthright son.

Whether Esau saw this as an opportunity to override the contract he had made earlier with his younger brother is not made clear. It is clear, however, that he fully intended to follow his father's instruction and receive the blessing.

Rebekah learned of all that was proceeding, and remembering the revelation she had received while she still carried her two sons in her womb, acted quickly. Contriving a plan to assure Jacob of his rightful blessing, Rebekah helped her son to effect a benign deception on the aging Isaac. The detailed account is one of the most fascinating episodes in the Old Testament record. It can be studied in its entirety in the 27th chapter of Genesis.

Rebekah's subterfuge was successful, and while Esau was still in the field hunting for his father's venison, Isaac was persuaded to give the blessing he had intended for Esau to the younger of the two brothers.

Significant in the blessing is the following:

"Therefore God give thee of the dew of heaven, and the fatness of the earth, and plenty of corn and wine.

"Let people serve thee, and nations bow down to thee: be lord over thy brethren, and let thy mother's sons bow down to thee..." (Gen. 27:28, 29).

When Esau returned and discovered his brother had deprived him of the blessing he had hoped to receive, he was enraged and vowed to take Jacob's life. Rebekah learned of Esau's intent and convinced Jacob that he should escape his brother's wrath by staying for a time with her family and kindred in Haran.

Isaac became reconciled to the well-intended deception that had been worked upon him. He called Jacob to him, charged him to take a wife from the family of Rebekah's brother Laban, and then gave him the following blessing:

"And God Almighty bless thee, and make thee fruitful, and multiply thee, that thou mayest be a multitude of people:

"And give thee the blessing of Abraham, to thee and to thy seed with thee, that thou mayest inherit the land wherein thou art a stranger, which God gave to Abraham" (Gen. 28:3, 4).

As Jacob traveled to Haran, both to choose a wife and to escape the threat of Esau's vow, he had a dream in which he saw the Lord, and the Lord spoke to him:

"...I am Lord God of Abraham thy father, and the God of Isaac: the land whereon thou liest, to thee will I give it, and unto thy seed:

"And thy seed shall be as the dust of the earth, and thou shalt spread abroad to the west, and to the east, and to the north, and to the south: <u>and in thee and thy seed shall all the families of the earth be blessed</u>" (Gen. 28:13, 14).

Esau also became the head of a nation of people, the Edomites, who settled the land southeast of Palestine. No mention is made, however, of Esau's descendants being made partakers of the covenant of Abraham and Isaac. It is of interest to note that an emotional reconciliation took place between Jacob and Esau twenty years after Jacob's hasty departure for Haran. In succeeding generations, however, a great deal of animosity developed between the Edomites and the Israelites.

In Haran, Jacob was taken into the household of Laban. He was successful in obtaining not only one wife, but four. They were Leah and Rachael, the daughters of Laban. Additionally, each of these wives gave to Jacob one of her handmaidens in a marriage relationship. Each of these women, Leah, Rachael, Bilhah, and Zilpah bore children. To Leah were born six sons and one daughter. They were Reuben, Simeon, Levi, Judah, Issachar, Zebulun, and Dinah. Rachael bore Joseph and Benjamin and died giving birth to her last son.

From Bilhah, Rachel's handmaid, came Dan and Naphtali. Zilpah, Leah's maid, bore Gad and Asher.

Jacob spent twenty years in Haran. During this time, all of his sons except Benjamin were born. He acquired considerable possessions, and when he left Haran to return to his homeland under the Lord's direction, he was a wealthy man.

As Jacob made his return to Canaan, the Lord appeared to him and gave the following revelation:

"Thy name is Jacob: thy name shall not be called any more Jacob, but Israel shall be thy name; and he called his name Israel.

"And God said unto him, I am God Almighty: be fruitful and multiply; a nation and a company of nations shall be out of thee, and kings shall come out of thy loins.

"And the land which I gave to Abraham and Isaac, to thee will I give it, and to thy seed after thee will I give the land" (Gen. 35:10-12).

It is of great importance to note that the covenant God made individually with Abraham, Isaac and Jacob now extended to all of Jacob's sons. This is evidenced in the blessing given to Jacob by Isaac which has already been cited: "And God Almighty bless thee, and make thee fruitful, and multiply thee, that thou mayest be a multitude of people.

"And give thee the blessing of Abraham, to thee, and to thy seed with thee" (Gen. 28:3, 4).

The twelve sons of Jacob, or Israel, therefore became the heads of the "house of Israel," the Lord's covenant people – sometimes spoken of as the twelve tribes of Israel. They assumed all of the responsibilities inherent with the covenant. It was the Lord's expectation that they would qualify as a "holy nation" and a "peculiar people" – a "light to the Gentiles." This was the trust placed in them by the Lord. It was a trust that they did not always fulfill.

This abbreviated account does not include the detail of Jacob's adventures in Haran where he was subject to the connivances of Laban, his father-in-law. It also bypasses the remarkable events in the life of Joseph, which see him sold into Egypt as a slave by his jealous brothers, where he miraculously rose to become the governor of the land, second in authority only to Pharaoh. These chapters in the scriptural record are worthy of the closest study for a number of reasons. Their detail, however, is not significantly relevant to the purpose of this study. It is sufficient to note that the family of Jacob moved from Canaan to Egypt to escape the effects of a severe famine and to capitalize on the generous assistance afforded them by Joseph's loving care. In Egypt they became "a multitude of people" over a four hundred-year period. While they retained much of the cultural tradition of their forefathers, they drifted substantially from the exalted purpose for which the Lord had chosen them.

Two items related to this time period are relevant to future events in the history of Israel. One of these has to do with Reuben's disqualifying himself as the birthright son, a position he would have held by tradition as the eldest of the three brothers. Reuben committed a grievous moral sin with one of the concubines of Jacob, his father. He was rejected by the Lord as a consequence of his transgression. Reuben, it will be recalled, was the son of Leah, the first wife of Jacob. With Reuben's rejection as the inheritor of the birthright role, Joseph, the first son of the second wife, Rachael, assumed this significant position and responsibility.

Joseph, as Rachael's son, was favored in many ways by his father. Rachael had always been Jacob's dearest and most loved companion. At her death, Jacob transferred many of these tender feelings to her first-born son. His special concessions to Joseph led to a powerful jealousy among the other sons.

In his early years, Joseph was permitted by the Lord to have some premonition of his birthright role. He experienced two dreams in which he saw himself receiving obeisance from his brethren:

"And Joseph dreamed a dream, and he told it his brethren: and they hated him the more.

"And he said unto them, Hear, I pray you, this dream which I have dreamed:

"For behold, we were binding sheaves in the field, and, lo, my sheaf arose, and also stood upright: and, behold, your sheaves stood about and made obeisance to my sheaf" (Gen. 37:5-7).

Joseph's recounting of the dream was undoubtedly done in the innocence of his youth, but its effect on his brothers could not have been more devastating. "And his brethren said to him, Shalt thou indeed reign over us? and they hated him yet the more for his dreams, and for his words" (Gen. 37:8).

Joseph was unwise enough to tell his father and his brothers of another dream in which he saw the sun and the moon and eleven stars bowing down to him. Even Israel was offended by this account. It was largely as a result of these dreams and the jealousy and hatred which they fueled in his brothers' feelings that Joseph barely escaped death at their hands and was finally sold to a caravan as a slave.

There is also an intimation of the position of Joseph among the sons of Israel in the final blessing pronounced upon him by his father just prior to Israel's death: "Joseph is a fruitful bough, even a fruitful bough by a well; whose branches run over the wall:

"The archers have sorely grieved him, and shot at him, and hated him:

"But his bow abode in strength, and the arms of his hands were made strong by the hands of the Mighty God of Jacob: (from thence is the shepherd, the stone of Israel:)

"Even by the God of thy father, who shall help thee; and by the Almighty, who shall bless thee with blessings of heaven above, blessings of the deep that lieth under, blessings of the breasts, and of the womb:

"The blessings of thy father have prevailed above the blessings of my progenitors unto the utmost bound of the everlasting hills: <u>they shall be on the head of Joseph, and on the crown of the head of him that was separate from his brethren</u>" (Gen. 49:22-26).

The role of Joseph and his posterity among the tribes of Israel and the fulfillment of the Lord's promises to his people in the latter days makes this notation important.

The second item of interest has to do with Ephraim and Manasseh, the sons of Joseph, who assumed a status among the tribes of Israel equivalent to that of Jacob's own sons. In later years, as the people of Israel returned to the land of Canaan, the posterity of Ephraim and Manasseh received land inheritances and other considerations of status much as the other tribes. There was a reason for their receiving this special consideration.

Jacob and his household learned that Joseph was alive in Egypt and responded to his efforts to resettle them there during the time of the great famine. During this time, Jacob became acquainted with Joseph's two oldest sons who had been born while Joseph was separated from his father's family: "And Jacob said unto Joseph, God Almighty appeared to me at Luz in the land of Canaan, and blessed me,

"And he said unto me, Behold, I will make thee fruitful, and multiply thee, and I will make of thee a multitude of people; and will give this land to thy seed after thee for an everlasting possession.

"And now thy two sons, Ephraim and Manasseh, which were born unto thee in the land of Egypt, before I came unto thee into Egypt, are mine; as Reuben and Simeon, they shall be mine.

"And thy issue, which thou begettest after them, shall be thine, and shall be called after the name of their brethren in their inheritance" (Gen. 48:3-6).

Ephraim and Manasseh, then, were adopted by Jacob, or Israel, as his own sons. They were to assume a place equivalent in most respects to that of Reuben and Simeon and the other sons of Jacob.

Shortly before his death, Israel called Joseph to bring to him his sons so that he could pronounce a blessing upon them: "Now the eyes of Israel were dim for age, so that he could not see. And he brought them near unto him; and he kissed them and embraced them.

"And Israel said unto Joseph, I had not thought to see thy face: and, lo, God hath showed me also thy seed.

"And Joseph brought them out from between his knees, and he bowed himself with his face to the earth.

"And Joseph took them both, Ephraim in his right hand toward Israel's left hand, and Manasseh in his left hand toward Israel's right hand, and brought them near unto him" (Gen. 48:10-13).

In presenting his sons to Israel in this way, Joseph was following the custom and tradition of his people, for Manasseh was the older of the two boys and, in Joseph's mind, was to receive the blessing of the first-born – the birthright.

"And Israel stretched out his right hand, and laid it upon Ephraim's head, who was the younger, and his left hand upon Manasseh's head, guiding his hands wittingly for Manasseh was the firstborn.

"And he blessed Joseph, and said, God, before whom my fathers Abraham and Isaac did walk, the God which fed me all my life long unto this day.

"The Angel which redeemed me from all evil, bless the lads; and let my name be on them, and the name of my fathers, Abraham and Isaac; and let them grow into a multitude in the midst of the earth.

"When Joseph saw that his father laid his right hand upon the head of Ephraim, it displeased him; and he held up his father's hand, to remove it from Ephraim's head unto Manasseh's head.

"And Joseph said to his father, Not so, my father: for this is the firstborn; put thy right hand upon his head.

"And his father refused; and said, I know it, my son, I know it: he also shall become a people, and he also shall be great: but truly his younger brother shall be greater than he, and his seed shall become a multitude of nations.

"And he blessed them that day, saying, In thee shall Israel bless, saying, God make thee as Ephraim and Manasseh: and he set Ephraim before Manasseh" (Gen. 48:14-20).

This knowing departure by Israel from the traditional pattern of blessing also has significant ramifications for roles yet to be played by the posterity of these two sons of Joseph.

Israel died in Egypt, with a charge to his sons that he should be carried back to the land of Canaan and buried with his fathers. His body was embalmed by the Egyptians. Joseph saw that his father's wish was fulfilled.

Joseph lived to be one hundred and ten years old: "And Joseph said unto his brethren, I die: And God will surely visit you, and bring you out of this land unto the land which he sware to Abraham, to Isaac, and to Jacob.

"And Joseph took an oath of the children of Israel, saying, God will surely visit you, and ye shall carry up my bones from hence.

"So Joseph died, being an hundred and ten years old: and they embalmed him, and he was put in a coffin in Egypt" (Gen. 50:23-26).

So were laid anciently the foundations of the house of Israel.

CHAPTER 4
The Return to Canaan

Both Jacob and Joseph had made a promise that the people of Israel would one day return from Egypt to the land of Canaan. Joseph had said "...God will surely visit you, and bring you out of this land unto the land which he sware to Abraham, to Isaac, and to Jacob" (Gen. 50:24).

It was many generations before this promise was realized. For more than four hundred years, the people of Israel remained in Egypt. As new kings arose among the Egyptians, the favored status that the people of Israel had known during the time of Joseph was dramatically changed. Israel had increased in numbers to a point that they were regarded as a potential threat to the Egyptians.

"Now there arose up a new king over Egypt, which knew not Joseph.

"And he said unto his people, Behold, the people of the children of Israel are more and mightier than we:

"Come on, let us deal wisely with them; lest they multiply, and it come to pass, that, when there falleth out any way, they also join unto our enemies, and fight against us..."

"Therefore they did set over them taskmasters to afflict them with their burdens..."

"And they made their lives bitter with hard bondage" (Exodus 1:8-11, 13, 14).

These were the circumstances of the people of Israel until the time of Moses. Moses, it will be recalled, had been raised a prince in the house of the Pharaoh. He had been born into the tribe of Levi at a time when the male children who were born to Israelitish women were killed as a consequence of a royal decree in an effort to curtail the population growth of the house of Israel. Moses, as an infant, was set adrift on the Nile River on a raft of reeds. He was discovered by a daughter of Pharaoh who reared him as her own child.

Moses was undoubtedly aware of his Israelitish heritage, for his own mother had been employed as his nurse and care-giver. As he reached maturity, he must have been troubled by the circumstances of his people. On one occasion, he came upon an Egyptian guard who was ruthlessly abusing an Israelite slave. Moses killed the guard and buried him in the sand.

When Moses learned that the slaying of the Egyptian guard had been discovered, he feared for his own life. He fled from Egypt to the land of Midian where he was taken in by a Midianite family. The head of this family, whose name was Jethro, gave one of his daughters to Moses as his wife. Her name was Zipporah.

As the years passed the bondage of the Israelites in Egypt became more severe: "...the children of Israel sighed by reason of the bondage, and they cried, and their cry came up unto God by reason of the bondage.

"And God heard their groaning, and God remembered his covenant with Abraham, with Isaac, and with Jacob.

"And God looked upon the children of Israel and had respect unto them" (Exodus 2:23-25).

God called upon Moses, the Levite, to act as the instrument to free the people of Israel from their suffering:

"...I am the God of thy father, the God of Abraham, the God of Isaac, and the God of Jacob.

"...I have surely seen the affliction of my people which are in Egypt, and have heard their cry by reason of their taskmasters; for I know their sorrows" (Exodus 3:6,7).

"Come now therefore, and I will send thee unto Pharaoh, that thou mayest bring forth my people the children of Israel out of the land of Egypt" (Exodus 3:10).

"And I will take you to me for a people, and I will be unto you a God: and ye shall know that I am the Lord your God...

"And I will bring you unto the land, concerning the which I did swear to give it to Abraham, to Isaac, and to Jacob; and I will give it to you for an inheritance: I am the Lord" (Exodus 6:2-4, 6-8).

The miraculous power manifest through Moses in delivering the Israelites from their Egyptian bondage became the subject of song and legend among the people of Israel. Six hundred thousand men, besides women and children (see Exodus 12:37, 38), along with all their cattle and possessions, departed from the land of their captivity into the wilderness of Sinai.

Through Moses and his brother Aaron, the Lord instructed the people of Israel concerning the course they would need to follow to be restored to their promised role as heirs to the covenant.

The four hundred years among the Egyptians had produced a spiritual apathy and an absence of incentive and motivation. The Israelites had barely lost sight of their Egyptian taskmasters when they began to complain against Moses and the Lord. Not even when daily sustenance in the form of manna was provided for them did the people acknowledge God's goodness in their behalf.

The Lord's efforts to lift the people of Israel to the spiritual level that would qualify them once again for their chosen role won little response. At one point, after the people had created a golden calf to worship, the Lord's patience with them reached its limit: "And the Lord said unto Moses, I have seen this people, and, behold, it is a stiffnecked people:

"Now therefore let me alone, that my wrath may wax hot against them, and that I may consume them: and I will make of thee a great nation" (Exodus 32:9,10).

It appears that it was the Lord's intent to destroy the people altogether in consequence of their unresponsiveness and rebellion, and to raise up a new covenant group as Moses' seed. Moses, however, reasoned with the Lord and won an extension of divine forbearance. Moses was commanded to give to the people a lesser law, one that required obedience to many outward forms and performances. This law was to serve as a means for eventually lifting the people to a level of faith and obedience that would allow them to live the higher law of the gospel of Christ.

The Apostle Paul, in the meridian of times, reflected upon the purpose of the law that was given to Israel through Moses, and which became known as the law of Moses. Paul explained: "Wherefore the law was our schoolmaster to bring us unto Christ, that we might be justified by faith" (Galatians 3:24).

Moses' own patience with his people was tested to its limit: "And Moses returned unto the Lord, and said, Oh, this people have sinned a great sin...

"Yet now, if thou wilt forgive their sin–; and if not, blot me, I pray thee, out of thy book which thou hast written.

"And the Lord said unto Moses, whosoever hath sinned against me, him will I blot out of my book.

"Therefore now go, lead the people unto the place of which I have spoken unto thee: behold, mine angel shall go before thee: nevertheless in the day when I visit, I will visit their sin upon them (Exodus 32:31-34).

It required forty years to prepare the people of Israel for their promised reentry into the land of Canaan. During that forty years, they were required to wander in the wilderness of Sinai while an entire generation passed away. It would be a new generation whom the Lord would establish in the land of promise.

Several noteworthy events occurred while the people of Israel were in the wilderness that focus directly upon the central purpose of this writing. One of these has to do with the establishment of priesthood authority which gave order and direction to the affairs of the people. The Lord directed Moses: "And take thou unto thee Aaron thy brother, and his sons with him, from among the children of Israel, that he may minister unto me in the priest's office, even Aaron, Nadab and Abihu, Eleazar and Ithamar, Aaron's sons" (Exodus 28:1).

Thus was initiated the priesthood authority under which the lesser law given through Moses would be administered. This priesthood order became known as the Priesthood of Aaron, or the Aaronic Priesthood. Since Moses and Aaron were of the tribe of Levi, the name "Levitical" has also been applied at times to this priesthood order. The tribe of Levi, therefore, assumed the responsibility for ministering all of the ordinances and performances that were required under the Mosaic law. It must be remembered that this was to have a "schoolmaster" effect upon the people of Israel.

The Aaronic or Levitical Priesthood was to continue to be the legitimate source of authority among Israel until the time the Savior would undertake his earthly ministry. John the Baptist officiated under the auspices of this priesthood and held the administering keys of authority for the same.

Another significant development occurred during Israel's sojourn in the wilderness. The Lord commanded Moses to construct a portable tabernacle that would become the center of religious worship. It was in conjunction with this tabernacle that the ordinances of the Law of Moses were administered. It was the holy place where the Lord's presence was on occasion made manifest. The tabernacle was the forerunner for the temple that would one day be built in Jerusalem, and, in the "schoolmaster" context, it prepared the people to look forward to the central place the temple would fill in their spiritual lives.

Moses was not permitted to lead his people into the land of Canaan. When the time finally came to cross the river Jordan into the land of promise, Joshua assumed the role of leadership under the Lord's direction. To Joshua the Lord said: "...as I was with Moses, so shall I be with thee: I will not fail thee, nor forsake thee.

"Be strong and of good courage: for unto this people shalt thou divide an inheritance in the land, which I sware unto their fathers to give them" (Joshua 1:5, 6).

Before Moses was separated from his people, he gave them a charge which has great significance for the house of Israel. It is worth citing Moses' instructions in some detail:

"Hear, O Israel: The Lord our God is one Lord:

"And thou shalt love the Lord thy God with all thine heart, and with all thy soul, and with all thy might.

"And these words, which I command thee this day, shall be in thine heart:

"And thou shalt teach them diligently unto thy children, and shalt talk of them when thou sittest in thine house, and when thou walkest by the way, and when thou liest down, and when thou risest up.

"And thou shalt bind them for a sign upon thine hand, and they shall be as frontlets between thine eyes.

"And thou shalt write them upon the posts of thy house, and on thy gates.

"And it shall be, when the Lord thy God shall have brought thee into the land which he sware unto thy fathers, to Abraham, to Isaac, and to Jacob, to give thee great and goodly cities, which thou buildest not,

"And houses full of all good things, which thou filledst not, and wells digged, that thou diggedst not, vineyards and olive trees, which thou plantedst not; when thou shalt have eaten and be full;

"Then beware lest thou forget the Lord, which brought thee forth out of the land of Egypt, from the house of bondage" (Deut. 6:4-12).

"For the Lord thy God bringeth thee into a good land, a land of brooks of water, of fountains and depths that spring out of valleys and hills;

"A land of wheat, and barley, and vines, and fig trees, and pomegranates; a land of oil olive, and honey;

"A land wherein thou shalt eat bread without scarceness, thou shalt not lack anything in it; a land whose stones are iron, and out of whose hills thou mayest dig brass.

"When thou hast eaten and art full, then thou shalt bless the Lord thy God for the good land which he hath given thee.

"Beware that thou forget not the Lord thy God, in not keeping his commandments, and his judgments, and his statutes, which I command thee this day:

"Lest when thou hast eaten and art full, and hast built goodly houses, and dwelt therein;

"And when thy herds and thy flocks multiply, and thy silver and thy gold is multiplied, and all that thou hast is multiplied;

"Then thine heart be lifted up, and thou forget the Lord thy God, which brought thee forth out of the land of Egypt, from the house of bondage;"

"And thou say in thine heart, my power and the might of mine hand hath gotten me this wealth" (Deut. 8:7-14, 17).

This strong counsel given by Moses can well be applied to the people of Israel in all their generations. It was particularly fitting for those who were about to enter a land from which they had been absent for more than four hundred years. The homes, the vineyards, the cities that had been developed by the inhabitants of the land were now to fall into the hands of Israel by the Lord's decree. It was a time for sobering counsel as well as for rejoicing. The stage was set for the people of the covenant to be established in such a way that the Lord could demonstrate through them how he prospers and blesses in every way those who will worship him in truth and honor his covenant with them.

There is a prophetic note in the warning that Moses gave to his people who had been so erratic in their behavior during the forty years under his leadership:

"Take heed unto yourselves, lest ye forget the covenant of the Lord your God, which he made with you, and make you a graven image, or the likeness of anything, which the Lord thy God hath forbidden thee.

"For the Lord thy God is a consuming fire, even a jealous God.

"When thou shalt beget children, and ye shall have remained long in the land, and shall corrupt yourselves, and make a graven image, or the likeness of any thing, and shall do evil in the sight of the Lord thy God to provoke him to anger:

"I call heaven and earth to witness against you this day, that ye shall soon utterly perish from off the land whereunto ye go over Jordan to possess it; ye shall not prolong your days upon it, but shall utterly be destroyed.

"And the Lord shall scatter you among the nations, and ye shall be left few in number among the heathen, whither the Lord shall lead you.

"And there ye shall serve gods, the work of men's hands, wood and stone, which neither see, nor hear, nor eat, nor smell" (Deut. 4:23-28).

History has confirmed the events to which Moses alluded in this final counsel to his people. Israel would indeed suffer again for their fractious inclinations. But they would also enjoy a golden period of prosperity, power, and political dominance that would have been difficult for them to imagine as they struggled through their afflictions in the wilderness.

With Joshua at their head, the hosts of Israel crossed over Jordan into the land of Canaan.

CHAPTER 5

A Time of Chastening and Emerging

With the strength of the Lord to sustain them, Israel took possession of the land. The people who had come into Canaan during Israel's absence were largely displaced or destroyed. In all, thirty-three kings were conquered, and their cities and lands were occupied by the twelve tribes. Under the Lord's direction, Joshua divided the land among the tribes, each tribe receiving a geographical inheritance, except for Levi, whose duty it was to minister in the priest's office: "Only unto the tribe of Levi he gave none inheritance; the sacrifices of the Lord God of Israel made by fire are their inheritance..." (Joshua 13:14).

"...therefore they gave no part unto the Levites in the land, save cities to dwell in, with their suburbs for their cattle and their substance" (Joshua 14:4).

Ephraim and Manasseh, who had been adopted as Jacob's own sons in Egypt, each received an individual inheritance: "For the children of Joseph were two tribes, Manasseh and Ephraim..." (Joshua 14:4).

Before Joshua's death, he called all of the tribes of Israel before him to give his final counsel and instruction, just as Moses had. He said: "And behold, this day I am going the way of all the earth: and ye know in your hearts and in all your souls, that not one thing hath failed of all the good things which the Lord your God spake concerning you; all are come to pass unto you, and not one thing hath failed thereof" (Joshua 23:14).

"Now therefore fear the Lord, and serve him in sincerity and in truth: and put away the gods which your fathers served on the other side of the flood, and in Egypt, and serve ye the Lord" (Joshua 24:14).

"And the people answered and said, God forbid that we should forsake the Lord, to serve other gods;

"For the Lord our God, He it is that brought us up and our fathers out of the land of Egypt, from the house of bondage, and which did those great signs in our sight, and preserved us in all the way wherein we went, and among all the people through whom we passed" (Joshua 24:16-17).

As Moses had counseled, Joshua warned the people: "If ye forsake the Lord, and serve strange gods, then he will turn and do you hurt, and consume you, after he hath done you good" (Joshua 24:20).

The positive resolve felt by the people at the time of Joshua's passing was not sustained for long. There were still some hard lessons for them to learn before they could qualify for the special status the Lord had in mind for them. It was not long until they were worshipping the gods of the people whom they had conquered. Contention also developed among the various tribes. The words of the Lord came to the people: "I made you go up out of the land of Egypt, and have brought you unto the land which I sware unto your fathers; and I said, I will never break my covenant with you.

"And ye shall make no league with the inhabitants of this land; ye shall throw down their altars: but ye have not obeyed my voice: why have ye done this?

"Wherefore I also said, I will not drive them out from before you; but they shall be as thorns in your sides, and their gods shall be a snare unto you.

"And it came to pass...that the people lifted up their voice and wept" (Judges 2:1-4).

"And when Joshua had let the people go, the people of Israel went every man into his inheritance to possess the land.

"And the people served the Lord all the days of Joshua, and all the days of the elders that outlived Joshua, who had seen all the great works of the Lord, that he did for Israel.

"And Joshua the son of Nun, the servant of the Lord, died, being an hundred and ten years old.

"And they buried him in the border of his inheritance in Timnatheres, in the mount of Ephraim, on the north side of the hill Gaash.

"And also all that generation were gathered unto their fathers: and there arose another generation after them, which knew not the Lord, nor yet the works he had done for Israel" (Judges 2:6-10).

In their wickedness, the strength of the Lord withdrew from Israel, and it was not long before the Canaanites, the Philistines, the Midianites and others were harassing them and bringing them under subjection. From time to time, a righteous leader would arise under whose influence the people would qualify for the Lord's help and blessing, but for several generations the Israelites lacked spiritual stability. They bore the consequences of their wantonness.

In the days of Samuel, the prophet, Israel was united once again, and for a time they freed themselves from the bondage of the Philistines. In defiance of the Lord's counsel, however, they insisted on having a king rule over them: "And Samuel told all the words of the Lord unto the people that asked of him a king.

"And he said, This will be the manner of the king that shall reign over you: He will take your sons, and appoint them for himself, for his chariots, and to be his horsemen; and some shall run before his chariots.

"And he will appoint him captains over thousands, and captains over fifties; and will set them to ear his ground, and to reap his harvest, and to make his instruments of war, and instruments of his chariots.

"And he will take your daughters to be confectioneries, and to be cooks, and to be bakers.

"And he will take your fields, and your vineyards, and your olive yards, even the best of them, and give them to his servants" (1 Samuel 8:10-14).

"And ye shall cry out in that day because of your king which ye shall have chosen you; and the Lord will not hear you in that day.

"Nevertheless the people refused to obey the voice of Samuel; and they said, Nay; but we will have a king over us" (1 Samuel 8:18, 19).

As we look back upon this time in Israel's history, we wonder at their intransigence in defiance of the Lord's counsel and their apparent inability or unwillingness to learn from harsh experience. We marvel also at the Lord's patience with these people in whom he had placed such great trust, who consistently fell short of their spiritual privileges and responsibilities, and who refused to see and understand the role ascribed to them in the Lord's plan. As we reflect on their experiences, we must not be oblivious to the challenges of our own day and the proclivity that has too often been demonstrated by the Lord's covenant people to set aside his counsels and seek after the forbidden things of the world.

Saul, the son of Kish, a Benjamanite, was anointed King of Israel. For a time Israel prospered under their new king, but it was not long until the misfortunes prophesied by Samuel began to materialize. Saul became arrogant in his military successes and even took upon himself the offering of a sacrifice, a rite reserved for the priests of the tribe of Levi.

"So Saul took the kingdom over Israel, and fought against all his enemies on every side...(1 Samuel 14:47).

"And there was sore war against the Philistines all the days of Saul; and when Saul saw any strong man, or any valiant man, he took him unto himself" (1 Samuel 14:52).

Because of Saul's repeated acts of defiance against the Lord's counsel, he was rejected by the Lord. His power over Israel's enemies began to fail, and he faced a new threat from the Philistine armies.

It was in this circumstance that David, the son of Jesse, appeared on the scene and won immediate acclaim from all of Israel through his conquest of the Philistine giant Goliath. David was appointed the leader of the armies of Israel by Saul, and he took one of Saul's daughters as his wife.

David's popularity with the people aroused the jealousy of Saul, who determined to kill David and remove this apparent threat to his throne. For a period of time David's life was in jeopardy, but Saul and his three sons were killed in a battle with the Philistines. David was anointed king of Judah, and, after overcoming the opposition of the forces who were loyal to Saul, he was anointed king over all of Israel.

It was during David's reign that the kingdom of Israel reached the status of a regional power: "And David reigned over all Israel; and David executed judgment and justice unto all his people" (2 Samuel 8:15). The most powerful enemies of Israel were conquered by David and his armies, and they gave obeisance to Israel.

The great tragedy in David's life came as he succumbed to the temptation to take the wife of one of his captains. He became guilty not only of adultery, but of murder as well. From the time of David's transgression, the kingdom became plagued once again with inner strife and insurrection. Even David's own son, Absalom, sought to overthrow his father and take the kingdom for himself.

As David became old, he had his son Solomon anointed king: "And Solomon loved the Lord, walking in the statutes of David his father..." (1 Kings 3:3).

"...the Lord appeared to Solomon in a dream by night: and God said, Ask what I shall give thee.

"And Solomon said, Thou hast showed unto thy servant David my father great mercy, according as he walked before thee in truth, and in righteousness, and in uprightness of heart with thee; and thou hast kept for him this great kindness, that thou hast given him a son to sit on his throne, as it is this day. And now, O Lord my God, thou hast made thy servant king instead of David my father: and I am but a little child: I know not how to go out or come in.

"And thy servant is in the midst of thy people which thou hast chosen, a great people, that cannot be numbered nor counted for multitude.

"Give therefore thy servant an understanding heart to judge thy people, that I may discern between good and bad: for who is able to judge this so great a people?

"And the speech pleased the Lord, that Solomon had asked this thing.

"And God said unto him, Because thou hast asked this thing, and hast not asked for thyself long life; neither hast asked riches for thyself, nor hast asked the life of thine enemies; but hast asked for thyself understanding to discern judgment;

"Behold, I have done according to thy words: lo, I have given thee a wise and an understanding heart; so that there was none like thee before thee, neither after thee shall any arise like unto thee.

"And I have also given thee that which thou hast not asked, both riches and honor; so that there shall not be any among the kings like unto thee all thy days" (1 Kings 3:5-13).

As long as Solomon maintained his humility and his reliance upon the Lord, the marvelous blessings promised to him were his. The kingdom of Israel rose to its highest apex of power and influence under his rule.

"And God gave Solomon wisdom and understanding exceeding much, and largeness of heart...

"And Solomon's wisdom excelled the wisdom of all the children of the east country, and all the wisdom of Egypt" (1 Kings 4:29-30).

"And there came of all people to hear the wisdom of Solomon, from all the kings of the earth which had heard of his wisdom" (1 Kings 4:34).

It was during Solomon's reign that the great temple in Jerusalem was built: "And the word of the Lord came to Solomon, saying,

"Concerning this house which thou art in building, if thou wilt walk in my statutes, and execute my judgments, and keep all my commandments to walk in them; then will I perform my word with thee, which I spake unto David thy father:

"And I will dwell among the children of Israel, and will not forsake my people Israel" (1 Kings 6:11-13).

The temple was completed and dedicated by Solomon. In his dedicatory prayer, Solomon predicted events that would befall Israel subsequent to his own lifetime, even to the latter-day period. Solomon prayed concerning his people: "If they sin against thee, (for there is no man that sinneth not,) and thou be angry with them, and deliver them to the enemy, so that they carry them away captives unto the land of the enemy, far or near;

"Yet if they shall bethink themselves in the land of them that carried them captives, and repent, and make supplication unto thee in the land of them that carried them captives, saying, We have sinned, and have done perversely, we have committed wickedness;

"And so return unto thee with all their heart, and with all their soul, in the land of their enemies, which led them away captive, and pray unto thee toward their land, which thou gavest unto their fathers, the city which thou hast chosen, and the house which I have built for thy name:

"Then hear thou their prayer and their supplication in heaven thy dwelling place, and maintain their cause,

"And forgive thy people that have sinned against thee, and all their transgressions wherein they have transgressed against thee, and give them compassion before them who carried them captive, that they may have compassion on them:

"For they be thy people, and thine inheritance..." (1 Kings 8:46-51).

Following the dedication of the temple, the Lord appeared to Solomon and gave him a promise and a warning:

"And the Lord said unto him, I have heard thy prayer and thy supplication, that thou hast made before me: I have hallowed this house which thou hast built, to put my name there forever; and mine eyes and mine heart shall be there perpetually.

"And if thou wilt walk before me, as David thy father walked, in integrity of heart, and in uprightness, to do according to all that I have commanded thee, and wilt keep my statutes and my judgments:

"Then I will establish thy throne upon Israel forever, as I promised to David thy father, saying, There shall not fail thee a man upon the throne of Israel.

"But if ye shall at all turn from following me, ye or your children, and will not keep my commandments and my statutes which I have set before you, but go and serve other gods, and worship them:

"Then I will cut off Israel out of the land which I have given them; and this house, which I have hallowed for my name, will I cast out of my sight; and Israel shall be a proverb and a byword among all people" (1 Kings 9:2-7).

The warning given by the Lord was not heeded. Solomon married wives who were not of Israel, and who turned his heart and the hearts of the people of Israel to the worship of false gods. Once again the kingdom was torn with internal strife.

After forty years as king of a united Israel, Solomon died, and his son Rehoboam was anointed as king. Rehoboam laid heavy burdens of taxation upon the people and ruled with the hand of tyranny. A spirit of revolt grew among the people.

Jeroboam, an Ephraimite and a popular leader, had been appointed by Solomon over the house of Joseph. He became a spokesman for the people in their protests against the heavy burdens laid upon them by Rehoboam. When Rehoboam spurned the pleas of the people, a revolt occurred. Only the tribe of Judah and part of the tribe of Benjamin remained loyal to Rehoboam. The other tribes acknowledged Jeroboam as their king, and the kingdom was divided. The northernmost part, which was inhabited largely by the ten tribes who declared allegiance to Jeroboam, retained the designation of the kingdom of Israel. Those who remained loyal to Rehoboam became known as the kingdom of Judah. The kingdom of Israel had its capital at Samaria. Because Ephraimites were most prominent among the leaders of this group, it was also referred to at times as the kingdom of Ephraim. Judah had Jerusalem as its capital.

Under Jeroboam's rule, the people of Israel turned almost entirely to the worship of idols. In spite of the efforts of such notable prophets as Elijah the Tishhite and Amos, the kingdom fell into total apostasy. After a history of about 200 years under nineteen different kings, the northern kingdom was overrun and conquered by the Assyrians under Sennacherib sometime before 700 B.C. The ten tribes of Israel who comprised the kingdom were carried away as captives, and their identity has become obscured. They are known today as the lost tribes of Israel.

The southern kingdom of Judah remained somewhat more faithful to the worship of the Lord, due in large measure to some of the faithful kings such as Hezekiah and Josiah who came to power from time to time. It continued to remain intact for 135 years after the fall of the northern kingdom. However, the worship of false gods eventually led to apostasy. About 600 years before the birth of Christ, the kingdom of Judah fell to the Babylonians under King Nebuchadnezzar. Many of the leaders as well as the people were carried away as captives to Babylon.

Thus came to a close a remarkable period in the history of the covenant people. While they served the Lord and kept his commandments, they were blessed above all people. They asserted a powerful influence upon contemporary kingdoms. But as they rejected the Lord and betrayed the trust that had been placed in them, they suffered the consequences of their folly precisely as the Lord and his prophets had foretold.

CHAPTER 6

The Fall and Dispersion of Israel

In the declining days of the kingdoms of Israel and Judah, many prophets went among the people to warn them of impending tragedy if they would not repent and obey the terms of their covenant with God. We are indebted to the house of Judah for preserving a record of that time. All of the Old Testament record, in fact, has been passed to us through the tribe of Judah. That the Old Testament does not include all of the prophetic writings of the period is attested to in the Book of Mormon, where reference is made to at least three significant record keepers, Zenos, Zenock and Neum (see 1 Nephi 19:10).

It appears that the brass plates acquired by Lehi and his family from Laban, the keeper of the sacred records in Jerusalem, (see 1 Nephi 3:4), contained some of the writings of these men. The illuminating allegory of the olive tree, which comprises the 5th chapter of Jacob, is a direct extract from the writings of Zenos. It provides insights into the scattering and ultimate gathering of Israel that are invaluable, and to which considerable reference will be made in this chapter as well as others that follow.

Isaiah, Jeremiah, and Ezekial are three of the prominent Old Testament prophets whose lifetimes covered the period of the conquests of Israel and Judah. They give us a clear view of the conditions among these two kingdoms which led to their being overcome by the nations of Assyria and Babylon. All of these prophets also looked ahead to a time when the Lord would restore the house of Israel to the role and purpose intended for the covenant people.

Other records were kept by the people of Judah during the time of their captivity and their eventual return to Jerusalem, (see Nehemiah, Haggai, Zechariah), but there is little recorded of the events that occurred during the 400-year period preceding the Savior's birth.

The tribes of the Kingdom of Israel were also to keep records following their captivity. None of these are presently available to us, but the day will come when they will appear as part of the sacred history of the house of Israel. Nephi recorded in the Book of Mormon: "And it shall come to pass that the Jews shall have the words of the Nephites, and the Nephites shall have the words of the Jews; and the Nephites and the Jews shall have the words of the lost tribes of Israel..." (2 Nephi 29:13).

Isaiah, Jeremiah, Amos and Ezekial lamented the depths of iniquity into which the people of Israel had fallen: "Hear O heavens and give ear, O earth," wrote Isaiah, "for the Lord hath spoken, I have nourished and brought up children, and they have rebelled against me" (Isaiah 1:2).

"O Assyrian, the rod of mine anger, and the staff in their hand is my indignation.

"I will send him against an hypocritical nation, and against the people of my wrath will I give him charge, to take the spoil, and to take the prey, and to tread them down like the mire of the streets" (Isaiah 10:5-6).

The Lord's patience with Israel was exhausted, and it was time for them to be severely chastened:

"...This is a rebellious people," he said, "lying children, children that will not hear the law of the Lord.

"Which say to the seers, See not; and to the prophets, Prophesy not unto us right things, speak unto us smooth things, prophesy deceits" (Isaiah 30:9-10).

"O that thou hadst hearkened to my commandments! then had thy peace been as a river, and thy righteousness as the waves of the sea" (Isaiah 48:18).

Jeremiah recorded: "The Lord said also unto me in the days of Josiah the king, Hast thou seen that which backsliding Israel hath done? she is gone up upon every high mountain and under every green tree, and there hath played the harlot" (Jer. 3:6).

"But this people hath a revolting and a rebellious heart; and they are revolted and gone" (Jer. 5:23).

Jeremiah spoke the words of the Lord to the people of Judah: "And I will cast you out of my sight, as I have cast out all your brethren, even the whole seed of Ephraim" (Jer. 7:15).

"Israel is a scattered sheep; the lions have driven him away: first the king of Assyria hath devoured him; and last this Nebuchadnezzar, king of Babylon, hath broken his bones" (Jer. 50:17).

Ezekiel prophesied: "In all your dwelling places the cities shall be laid waste, and the high places shall be desolate; that your altars may be laid waste and made desolate, and your idols may be broken and cease, and your images may be cut down, and your works may be abolished.

"And the slain shall fall in the midst of you, and ye shall know that I am the Lord" (Ezekiel 6:6-7).

Israel was no longer qualified to inhabit the lands that had been given to them as an inheritance. They were to be scattered upon all the face of the earth for a season of chastisement. Many of them would be lost from the pages of history for a prolonged period. The fulfillment of the Lord's promise to his covenant people would await a later time.

The Book of Mormon record, and the latter-day revelations to the prophet Joseph Smith, shed some additional light on the scattering of Israel. We know that Lehi and his family, descendants of Manasseh (see Alma 10:3), who remained in Jerusalem after the division of the two kingdoms, were directed by the Lord to escape the destruction that was to come upon the city during the Babylonian invasion. Nephi,

Lehi's son, recorded: "And it came to pass that the Lord commanded my father, even in a dream, that he should take his family and depart into the wilderness" (1 Nephi 2:2).

The final days of King Zedekiah's reign had come. Lehi had joined with Jeremiah in warning the Jews of the devastation that awaited them unless they would repent: "And it came to pass that the Jews did mock him because of the things which he testified of them; for he truly testified of their wickedness and their abominations...

"And when the Jews heard these things they were angry with him; yeah, even as with the prophets of old, whom they had cast out, and stoned, and slain..." (1 Nephi 1:19, 20).

Lehi and his family were later joined by Ishmael, another Josephite, and his family. In at least partial fulfillment of Jacob's blessing to his son, Joseph, this group became part of Joseph's branches that would go "over the wall" (see Gen. 49:22). They were led eventually to the American continents where they became the foundation of a great Israelite nation in ancient America.

We know that a son of King Zedekiah, whose name was Mulek, was also directed to the Americas in this same time period. It is recorded in the book of Helaman: "Now the land south [in the Americas] was called Lehi, and the land north was called Mulek, which was after the son of Zedekiah; for the Lord did bring Mulek into the land north, and Lehi into the land south" (Hel. 6:10).

This same account in the Book of Mormon tells us that all of Zedekiah's sons, with the exception of Mulek, were killed as the Babylonians overran Jerusalem (see Hel. 8:21). Jeremiah confirms the death of all of the sons of Zedekiah who remained in Jerusalem: "And the king of Babylon slew the sons of Zedekiah before his eyes...

"Then he put out the eyes of Zedekiah" (Jer. 52:10, 11).

A unification of the people of Mulek with a branch of the descendants of Lehi occurred almost four hundred years after their arrival in the new world. The Mulekites under a king named Zarahemla joined with the Nephites under King Mosiah (see Omni

1:14-15, 19). Following this unification, both groups were known as Nephites. The union of this group of Josephites with the descendants of Mulek, who was of the house of Judah, may in part account for Nephi's statement in 2 Nephi 30:4: "And then shall the remnant of our seed know concerning us, how that we came out from Jerusalem, and that they are descendants of the Jews."

It is a great blessing to have included in the Book of Mormon a comprehensive record of this branch of the house of Israel, a record which covers the period from 600 B.C. to 400 A.D. Much more will be said about this people and their record.

We can learn a few important facts about those who have become known as the lost tribes of Israel by a careful review of the direct and indirect references made to them in the scriptures. Both Jeremiah and Isaiah speak of them as being in the "lands of the north" (see Jer. 16:15; 31:8 and Isaiah 49:12). The Lord also speaks of them in latter-day revelations as being in the north countries (see D&C 110:11; 133:26). Zenos' allegory of the olive tree in the fifth chapter of Jacob in the Book of Mormon relates in large part to these tribes. Zenos begins his allegory by referring to the spiritual decline of Israel and to their scattering in these terms: "For behold, thus saith the Lord, I will liken thee, O house of Israel unto a tame olive-tree, which a man took and nourished in his vineyard; and it grew and waxed old, and began to decay.

"And it came to pass that the Master of the vineyard went forth, and he saw that his olive-tree began to decay; and he said; I will prune it, and dig about it, and nourish it, that perhaps it may shoot forth young and tender branches, and it perish not" (Jacob 5:3, 4).

What better way to describe the drift of Israel into disobedience and the Lord's efforts to bring them to repentance and reformation. In Zenos' account, the exertions of the master of the vineyard prove to be unproductive. As a consequence, he determines to break off some of the branches and make grafts of them in other parts of the vineyard: "And behold, saith the Lord of the vineyard, I will take away many of these young and tender branches, and I will graft them whithersoever I will; and it mattereth not that if it so be that the root of this tree will perish, I may preserve the fruit thereof unto myself; wherefore, I will take these young and tender branches, and I will graft them whithersoever I will" (Jacob 5:8).

"And it came to pass that the Lord of the vineyard went his way, and hid the natural branches of the tame olive-tree in the nethermost parts of the vineyard, some in one and some in another, according to his will and pleasure" (Jacob 5:14).

Looking ahead to other periods of Israel's history which will be discussed in greater detail in later chapters, it is of importance to note several additional references in Zenos' word picture. "And it came to pass that a long time passed away..."(Jacob 5:15). The allegory now takes us to a period which appears, from other points of reference, to represent the meridian of times. The Master of the vineyard determines to go to the places where he has hidden the grafted branches to see how they are faring. The significant point of this account, in terms of Israel's scattering, is that the branches are still largely in the locations where they had been taken by the Lord in the earlier dispersion.

The fact of the Lord's visit to these scattered remnants in the meridian of times is confirmed in what he shared with the Nephite people concerning his charge from the Father to show himself to the "other sheep," following his resurrection (see 3 Nephi 16).

At a still later period (see Jacob 5:29), following a time of complete apostasy when the entire vineyard brings forth bad fruit, the Lord surveys once again the condition of those who have been transplanted, and, overall, they appear to be in the same locations (see Jacob 5:38-45).

As mentioned, a more detailed reference to Zenos' allegory will be made later in this writing. The point significant to Israel's scattering, and particularly to the lost tribes, is that throughout ensuing history they have largely remained in those places where the Lord took them at the time of their dispersion. They have lost their identity, both to themselves and to the world, as remnants of the Lord's covenant people, but they have been preserved as he had promised.

Others of the tribes would become scattered among all nations and among all peoples. This would be true of some who were initially carried away by the Assyrians as well as the Jews.

Nephi, while commenting upon references made by earlier prophets concerning the house of Israel, makes this significant note:

"Wherefore, the things of which I have read are things pertaining to things both temporal and spiritual; for it appears that the house of Israel, sooner or later, will be scattered upon all the face of the earth, and also among all nations.

"And behold, there are many who are already lost from the knowledge of those who are at Jerusalem. Yea, the more part of the tribe have been led away, and they are scattered to and fro upon the isles of the sea; and whither they are none of us knoweth, save that we know that they have been led away.

"...wherefore, they shall be scattered among all nations and shall be hated of all men" (1 Nephi 22:3-5).

Abraham was promised that one of the ways his seed was to be a blessing to all the families of the earth would be through the presence of his literal seed among all nations (see Abraham 2:9-10). In the scattering of Israel, the Lord brought a severe and much-deserved chastisement upon his covenant people; he also placed them in circumstances where they would yet fulfill the agent role that he had ascribed to them in the beginning. The Lord had not forsaken the promise made to Abraham and his seed. All that he has promised will yet be fulfilled.

CHAPTER 7

Israel in the Meridian of Times

We have no records of the tribes of the northern kingdom following their captivity by the Assyrians. The Book of Mormon is the record of the groups who came to the new world under the leadership of Lehi and Mulek.

The books of Ezra, Nehemiah, Esther, Daniel, Haggai and Zechariah are the work of writers and prophets who lived in the time following the Babylonian conquest of Judah. The Old Testament does not contain detailed historical information for a period of about 400 years preceding the birth of Christ.

During the Babylonian captivity of Judah, there were those among the Jews who rose to positions of eminence and influence among their captors. Daniel was one of these notables. His story was not unlike that of Joseph in Egypt. Through his faith and obedience to the laws of Jehovah, Daniel was given power to interpret dreams and visions and was blessed with great wisdom. He was called upon to interpret a dream of King Nebuchadnezzar when all the wise men and the sorcerers of the king had failed to do so. The dream itself is significant, for it has prophetic implications concerning the Lord's work among his people in the latter days (see Daniel 2:31-45).

Impressed with Daniel's powers, the king placed him in a position of power: "Then the king made Daniel a great man, and gave him many great gifts, and made him ruler over the whole province of Babylon, and chief of the governors over all the wise men of Babylon" (Daniel 2:48).

Daniel's influence among the royalty of Babylon continued until the time of Cyrus and Darius the king of Persia. He prophesied of the return of the Jews to Jerusalem and of the appearance of the Messiah through Jewish lineage (see Daniel 9:20-27). Ezra, Nehemiah, Haggai and Zechariah contain an account of the return of some of the Jews to Jerusalem under the reign of Cyrus. Zerubbabel, of the royal line of Judah, was appointed by Cyrus to be governor of Palestine. It was under his administration that the temple in Jerusalem was rebuilt, and a Jewish nation began to emerge once again in the Palestinian area.

Ezra, a priest and scribe among the Jews, was allowed to take to Jerusalem any of the Jewish exiles who desired to return. Nehemiah received permission to rebuild the walls of the city, which he accomplished in spite of much opposition.

With the return of the Jews to Palestine, the stage was set for the appearance of the Savior in his earthly ministry. Palestine would come under both Greek and Roman rule prior to the birth of Jesus. His birth and ministry among the Jews is well documented in the New Testament. Jewish tradition and the forecasting of their greatest prophets had established among this branch of the house of Israel the expectation that a Messiah would appear through the lineage of David. The many years of captivity and being subjected to the demeaning status of a conquered nation had led the Jews to look for a Messiah who would come in great power to overthrow their enemies and restore them to what they regarded as their rightful place of dominance and preeminence as the Lord's favored people.

The Savior's humble advent into mortality could hardly have been more divergent from the accepted tradition. His power was to be manifest in the dramatic conversion in the hearts and lives of individual people. He could rightfully say that his kingdom was not to be of this world. In order for his covenant people to fulfill their foreordained role, they would need to recognize the divine power in the love, compassion, integrity, obedience, faith and sacrifice of God's only begotten Son, commit themselves unreservedly to accept him as their Savior and Redeemer, and model his perfect example.

The Lord's declaration: "I am the way, the truth, and the life: no man cometh unto the Father, but by me" (John 14:6) left the Jews confused and unbelieving. When he promised: "I am the resurrection, and the life: he that believeth in me, though he were dead, yet shall he live: "And he that liveth and believeth in me shall never die" (John 11:26), the Jews were not ready to believe.

Only a relative handful saw clearly in the life of Jesus of Nazareth, the carpenter's son, the culmination of all of God's promises of salvation and exaltation for his children. The Maker of the Covenant had come to his covenant people, and they were not ready to receive him. When his disciples wondered why he did not turn to the Gentiles, he responded, "I am not sent but unto the lost sheep of the house of Israel" (Matt. 15:24).

On another occasion he disclosed: "And other sheep I have, which are not of this fold: them also I must bring, and they shall hear my voice; and there shall be one fold, and one shepherd" (John 10:16). When he later appeared as the resurrected Lord to the Nephites and Lamanites in the new world, he referenced this disclosure that he had made to the Jews:

"Ye are my disciples; and ye are a light unto this people, who are a remnant of the house of Joseph.

"And not at any time hath the Father given me commandment that I should tell it unto your brethren at Jerusalem.

"Neither hath the Father given me commandment that I should tell unto them concerning the other tribes of the house of Israel, whom the Father hath led away out of the land.

"This much did the Father command me, that I should tell unto them:

"That other sheep I have which are not of this fold; and them also I must bring, and they shall hear my voice; and there shall be one fold, and one shepherd.

"And now, because of stiff neckedness and unbelief they understood not my word; therefore, I was commanded to say no more of the Father concerning this thing unto them.

"But, verily, I say unto you that the Father hath commanded me, and I tell it unto you, that ye were separated from among them because of their iniquity; therefore it is because of their iniquity that they know not of you.

"And verily, I say unto you again that the other tribes hath the Father separated from them; and it is because of their iniquity that they know not of them.

"And verily, I say unto you, that ye are they of whom I said: Other sheep I have that are not of this fold; them also I must bring, and they shall hear my voice; and there shall be one fold, and one shepherd.

"And they understood me not, for they supposed it had been the Gentiles; for they understood not that the Gentiles should be converted through their preaching.

"And they understood me not that I said they shall hear my voice; and they understood me not, that the Gentiles should not at any time hear my voice – that I should not manifest myself unto them save it were by the Holy Ghost.

"But behold, ye have both heard my voice, and seen me; and ye are my sheep, and ye are numbered among those whom the Father hath given me" (3 Nephi 15:12, 14-24).

"And verily, verily, I say unto you that I have other sheep, which are not of this land, neither of the land of Jerusalem, neither in any parts of the land round about whither I have been to minister.

"For they of whom I speak are they who have not as yet heard my voice; neither have I at any time manifested myself unto them.

"But I have received a commandment of the Father that I shall go unto them; and that they shall hear my voice, and shall be numbered among my sheep, that there may be one fold and one shepherd; therefore, I go to show myself unto them.

"And I command you that ye shall write these sayings after I am gone, that if it so be that my people at Jerusalem, they who have seen me and been with me in my ministry, do not ask the Father in my name, that they may receive a knowledge of you by the Holy Ghost, and also of the other tribes whom they know not of, that these sayings which ye shall write shall be kept and shall be manifested unto the Gentiles, that through the fullness of the Gentiles, the remnant of their seed, who shall be scattered forth upon the face of the earth because of their unbelief, may be brought in, or may be brought to a knowledge of me, their Redeemer" (3 Nephi 16:1-4).

Several profoundly significant things are revealed in this instruction of the Savior to his "sheep" who were in the new world.

First: In his ministry to the Father's children in the meridian of times, he would focus his full attention upon those who were of the house of Israel – this by commandment of the Father. The promise made in God's covenant with Abraham would be honored; that is, it would be through Abraham's seed, "...that in their hands they shall bear this ministry and Priesthood unto all nations (Abraham 2:9). It would be through God's agent people, the house of Israel, that... "the Gentiles should be converted through their preaching" (3 Nephi 15:22).

Second: By the time of the Savior's appearance among the Jews, the house of Judah had apparently forgotten, at least in large measure, that God's covenant pertained to the people of all of the tribes of Israel, not just to the Jews. It had been into the tribe of Judah that the Savior had been born, but his ministry was to all of his "sheep" who were of the house of Israel.

Third: The resurrected Lord made himself manifest to the remnant of Jacob in the Americas whom he had separated from their brethren in Jerusalem 600 years earlier. He left with this branch of Israel the personal witness of his resurrection and the fact that he had overcome the power of death.

Fourth: The Lord was to manifest himself, by commandment of the Father, to the other branches of the house of Israel who had been led away and were lost to the world; he would show himself unto them, and they would hear his voice. They would receive the same personal witness and ministry that the Jews had received in Jerusalem, and that the remnant had received in the new world.

Fifth: A written record of these visits by the resurrected Savior to his covenant people was to be made and kept.

Sixth: In the meridian of time, the location of all of the tribes of Israel was known to the Lord, and his concern, as well as the concern of the Father, was as great for all as it was for one.

It is of great interest and significance that in the Zenos allegory, a clear reference is made to these visits of the Lord to his lost sheep (see Jacob 5:15-25). Further, there is the direct implication that, following these visits, there was a time of restoration among each of the branches, for in each case the branches for a time "brought forth much fruit" (Jacob 5:20).

It would not be unreasonable to assume that, just as in the case of the Nephites and Lamanites, the appearance of the resurrected Lord to these people would bring about a spiritual revival which would result in their enjoying the good fruits of the gospel in their lives for a time.

It is also of interest to note that in the report of these visits by the Savior to the branches which he had earlier grafted into trees in the "nethermost parts of his vineyard," Zenos makes reference to at least four distinct groups (see Jacob 5:20, 21, 24, 25).

We must await the day when the records of these people are available to us, as Nephi promised they would one day be (see 2 Nephi 29:13), to learn of the events that accompanied the Savior's visits to them. We know of the dramatic occurrences that took place in the new world in preparation for the appearance of the glorified Lord. Only the more righteous of the people were permitted to survive the devastating changes that took place as a prelude to the Savior's brief ministry among this branch of Israel (see 3 Nephi, chapters 8, 9, 10).

While he ministered among the Nephites and Lamanites, the Savior established his Church, appointed authorized servants to carry on his work, and directed them in initiating the essential ordinances of salvation, just as he had in Jerusalem.

Through all generations, the Father and the Son made manifest their love for all of God's children, and they made clear that the covenant established anciently with Abraham, Isaac, and Jacob was still in full force. The Savior in his mortal ministry fulfilled completely his purpose for coming to the earth. His infinite atonement extended to all the hope and promise of forgiveness for sins and transgressions, conditioned upon faith unto repentance. His overcoming of the power of death made the resurrection a reality for all mankind.

His perfect example and his teachings outlined the manner in which men may live in peace, love, and harmony. He made possible the salvation, exaltation and eternal life of all of God's children by removing for them every barrier to progress and development that they could not remove themselves. He came as Israel's king and lawgiver, and gave the assurance that every promise made to his covenant people would yet be fulfilled. The glorious period of the Lord's earthly ministry would eventually fade into the darkness of a universal apostasy. But shining through this darkness was the promise of a latter-day restoration and the eventual spiritual reawakening of the people of the covenant.

Part III

Israel in the Latter Days

CHAPTER 8

Who Are the House of Israel Today?

In the centuries that have passed since Abraham's day, tracing the identify and location of the people of the covenant has become an increasing challenge. Since so much that has been prophesied concerning them remains to be fulfilled, it is important to have some understanding of who they are today. The Jews have been so visible in recent historical events that many have come to regard them as the modern-day remnant of the house of Israel. While the part they are playing in current world affairs, and that which they will yet play is of great significance, it is essential to remember that they are only one branch of the covenant people.

The scriptures continue to be the most reliable source for establishing a present-day profile of the house of Israel. Since the tribe of Judah has already been mentioned, they may provide a good point of departure in our attempt to answer the question: "Who are the house of Israel today?"

Probably beginning with the Babylonian conquest, and certainly continuing during the time the Greeks and the Romans had political control over the Palestinian area, there is evidence that groups of Jewish people began to spread throughout the Mediterranean crescent and even beyond. One indication of this is found in the record of the missionary travels of the Apostle Paul and his companions. Wherever clusters of the Jewish people settled, they appeared to maintain a separate culture, tradition, and religious worship. In many of the principal cities of the Mediterranean area, Jewish synagogues were established. It was to these synagogues that Paul would go to initiate his missionary labors as he moved from city to city. Generally his first efforts in each of these locations were directed to the Jewish communities. Some of the cities where Paul found synagogues that are specifically mentioned in the book of Acts include Salamis and Paphos on the Island of Cyprus, Antioch of Pisidia, Iconium, Philippi in Macedonia, Thessalonica, Tarsus, Lystra, Derbe, Athens, Corinth, Ephesus, and Rome. Jewish settlements had also developed in the cities of Egypt.

In the Roman siege of Jerusalem by Titus in the first half-century following the death of Christ, a major scattering of the Jews began. By the Middle Ages, they were found in all of the major cities of Europe, and some had spread into Asia. In the modern period they have literally scattered to the four quarters of the earth.

In large measure, the Jewish people have maintained their racial identity, even though there has been some mixing with the peoples among whom they have settled in all parts of the world. The house of Judah, therefore, has a significant visible identity today. They represent one major segment of the house of Israel. Their efforts in recent years to gather once again to their homeland, and the establishment of the nation of Israel, have enhanced their visibility.

A second group who has maintained a degree of racial identity to the present day are the descendants of those who came to the new world with Lehi and with Mulek, whose record is found in the Book of Mormon. Lehi was a descendant of Joseph and Manasseh (Alma 10:3), while Mulek, a son of King Zedekiah, was of Judah (see Hel. 6:10; Mosiah 25:2). After a unification of the people of Lehi and the people of Mulek occurred, they were generally spoken of as being of the line of Joseph (see Alma 46:23, 24). Their descendants who have continued to the present day have been known as Lamanites (a Book of Mormon term), Indians, Native Americans, etc. They were the inhabitants of the American continents who were encountered when the settlement of North and South America by Europeans began in the 15th and 16th centuries.

This branch of the people of Joseph have become numerous today, in spite of heavy losses sustained in the conflicts which occurred during the early colonization of the Americas by those who came from other parts of the world. Tens of millions of the modern inhabitants of North America, Central America, and South America can claim in some measure the lineage of Joseph by virtue of their tie to the Book of Mormon peoples.

It should be pointed out with emphasis that these descendants of Joseph are the posterity of a mere handful of the tribe of Joseph who came to the new world about 600 B.C. under the Lord's direction. The major segment of Joseph's seed were among the ten northern tribes of the Kingdom of Israel when they were carried away captive by the Assyrians more than seven hundred years before the birth of Christ, and they became part of the lost tribes.

Lehi, the great prophet and patriarch of the remnant of Joseph who came to the new world, named his youngest son Joseph after their forbearer of old. In his final blessing to his last-born son, Lehi said: "And now, Joseph, my last-born, whom I have brought out of the wilderness of my afflictions, may the Lord bless thee forever, for thy seed shall not utterly be destroyed.

"For behold, thou art the fruit of my loins; and I am descendant of Joseph who was carried captive into Egypt. And great were the covenants of the Lord which he made unto Joseph.

"Wherefore, Joseph truly saw our day, and he obtained a promise of the Lord, that out of the fruit of his loins the Lord God would raise up a righteous branch unto the house of Israel; not the Messiah, but a branch which was to be broken off, nevertheless, to be remembered in the covenants of the Lord that the Messiah should be made manifest to them in the latter days, in the spirit of power, unto the bringing them out of darkness unto light..." (2 Nephi 3:3-5).

A second-known segment of the house of Israel in the present time, therefore, are the "native" inhabitants of the Americas, who are of the lineage of Joseph. To the great majority of these people their Israelitish heritage has been lost. In the years of apostasy from the Lord's law, which followed after his visit among them, these people forgot their identity as a branch of the house of Israel. However, a great reawakening is occurring as the gospel of Jesus Christ is once again being taken to them. Much is yet in store for these people as the Lord's promises to them are being fulfilled.

Nephi, the son of Lehi, prophesied of the time in the last days when the gospel of Christ and the message of the covenant would once again be taken to his people: "And at that day shall the remnant of our seed know that they are of the house of Israel, and that they are the covenant people of the Lord; and then shall they know and come to a knowledge of their forefathers; and also to the knowledge of the gospel of their Redeemer and the very points of his doctrine, that they may know how to come unto him and be saved."

"Behold, I say unto you, Yea; they shall be remembered again among the house of Israel; they shall be grafted in, being a natural branch of the olive-tree, into the true olive-tree" (1 Nephi 15:14-16).

Mormon, one of the last prophets among the Nephite people and their principal record keeper, knew that the day would come when the remnant of his people would receive the record which he had abridged and preserved. He addressed his final words to them:

"And now, behold, I would speak somewhat unto the remnant of this people who are spared, if it so be that God should give unto them my words, that they may know the things of their fathers; yea, I speak unto you, ye remnant of the house of Israel; and these are the words which I speak:

"Know ye that ye are of the house of Israel" (Mormon 7:1, 2).

Mormon's primary concern was that the descendants of his people would understand that they are the covenant people of the Lord.

A third segment of the house of Israel is that body which have become known as the lost tribes. They disappeared from the pages of history following their conquest by the Assyrians. Their location and their identity are unknown. The Zenos allegory of the olive tree in Jacob 5 in the Book of Mormon gives us some insights concerning these people. They were taken to the "nethermost parts of the vineyard, some in one and some in another...." (Jacob 5:14).

An interesting exchange takes place in the allegory between the Lord of the vineyard and a servant who accompanies him as they visit the places where the branches of the olive tree had been taken, after a "long time" had passed:

"And it came to pass that they went forth whither the Master had hid the natural branches of the tree, and he said unto the servant: Behold, these; and he beheld the first that it had brought forth much fruit...

"And it came to pass that the servant said unto his master: How comest thou hither to plant this tree, or this branch of the tree? For behold, it was the poorest spot in all the land of thy vineyard.

"And the Lord of the vineyard said unto him: Counsel me not; I knew it was a poor spot of ground..." (Jacob 5:20-22).

Then the Lord of the vineyard and his servant visits another location and he adds, "Look hither; behold I have planted another branch of the tree also; and thou knowest that this spot of ground was poorer than the first" (Jacob 5:23).

A third location is then visited, and the Lord says, "Look hither, and behold another branch also, which I have planted..." (Jacob 5:24).

Finally, the Lord and his servant visit a fourth location, and the Lord says to his servant: "Look hither and behold the last. Behold this I have planted in a good spot of ground..." (Jacob 5:25). From other information shared by the Lord with his servant, it appears the fourth branch which is visited has reference to the branch of Joseph (Lehi and his people) who came to the new world. This seems to be confirmed when, at a later time, the Master says, "And behold this last...I did plant in a good spot of ground; yea, even that which was choice unto me above all other parts of the land of my vineyard" (Jacob 5:43).

Jeremiah and Isaiah, when speaking of the lost tribes, often refer to them as being in the "land of the north" or the "north country" (see Jeremiah 16:15; 23:8; Isaiah 49:12).

When Joseph Smith and Oliver Cowdery were visited in the Kirtland Temple by heavenly messengers who conferred essential keys of authority upon them for various aspects of the Lord's work, they recorded: "...and Moses appeared before us, and committed unto us the keys of the gathering of Israel from the four parts of the earth, and the leading of the ten tribes from the land of the north" (D&C 110:11).

As the Lord revealed to Joseph Smith essential information concerning the coming of these same tribes to Zion in the last days, he said: "And they who are in the north countries shall come in remembrance before the Lord..." (D&C 133:26).

While we can do no more than speculate upon the whereabouts and identity of these people, it is significant to note that they are apparently still in a relatively coherent group; when they are moved upon to gather, they will move as a body, and they will, it appears, be a numerous company. As they come to Zion, the "boundaries of the everlasting hills shall tremble at their presence" (D&C 133:31). More of this fascinating subject will be discussed in the final chapter.

It appears that those who comprise the lost tribes are in much the same situation as were the Nephites and the Lamanites pertaining to the recognition of their identity with the tribes of Israel. But the time will come when "they shall come in remembrance before the Lord..." (D&C 133:26). It will be a memorable day.

A fourth group among the house of Israel today are represented by those who would be "scattered upon all the face of the earth, and also among all nations" (1 Nephi 22:3). As has been indicated, the Jews have certainly experienced a world-wide dispersion. But others of Israel have also dispersed to the "four parts of the earth." It perhaps bears repeating that in the covenant made with Abraham, God promised that "...in thy seed after thee (that is to say, the literal seed, or the seed of the body) shall all the families of the earth be blessed" (Abraham 2:11).

In some manner, through the physical presence of those who would be of Abraham's lineage, the Lord intends to bring blessings to people throughout the earth. This does not suggest that the blood of Israel would be found in all of the earth's inhabitants, but some of

Israelitish heritage would apparently become so broadly scattered upon the earth that they would be found in all nations. They would mix with the Gentiles and in many instances would be identified with the Gentiles.

The scriptural references to this segment of present-day Israel seem to distinguish clearly between them and the principal body of the ten tribes who would remain largely intact through generations. Note Joseph Smith's reference to them in D&C 110:11 which has already been cited: "Moses appeared before us, and committed unto us the keys of the gathering of Israel from the four parts of the earth, and the leading of the ten tribes from the land of the north." There is a clear distinction made between the ten tribes, who are still somewhere in the north lands, and those who would be scattered world-wide.

Isaiah also distinguishes between the scattered Jews and the other outcasts of Israel who will one day be gathered. "And he shall set up an ensign for the nations, and shall assemble the outcasts of Israel, and gather together the dispersed of Judah from the four corners of the earth.

"The envy also of Ephraim shall depart, and the adversaries of Judah shall be cut off: Ephraim shall not envy Judah, and Judah shall not vex Ephraim" (Isaiah 11:12, 13).

In this last verse there appears to be more than a slight inference that among those who would be scattered, apart from the Jews, Ephraim would be prominent. The prophet Zechariah seems to confirm the fact that the tribe of Ephraim would be scattered among the nations. He said, "And they of Ephraim shall be like a mighty man, and their heart shall rejoice as through wine: yea, their children shall see it, and be glad. Their heart shall rejoice in the Lord.

"I will hiss for them, and gather them for I have redeemed them: and they shall increase as they have increased.

"And I will sow them among the people: and they shall remember me in far countries; and they shall live with their children, and turn again.

"I will bring them again also out of the land of Egypt, and gather them out of Assyria; and I will bring them into the land of Gilead and Lebanon; and place shall not be found for them" (Zechariah 10:7-10).

This postulate will be developed further, for there is something in it of great significance.

Isaiah also acknowledges the mixing that would take place with this scattered group of Israel among the Gentiles: "And their seed shall be known among the Gentiles, and their offspring among the people: all that see them shall acknowledge them, that they are the seed which the Lord hath blessed" (Isaiah 61:9).

In the dedicatory prayer which he pronounced at the Kirtland Temple, Joseph Smith also acknowledges the masking of some of Israel among the Gentiles: "Now these words, O Lord, we have spoken before thee, concerning the revelations and commandments which thou hast given unto us, who are identified with the Gentiles" (D&C 109:60).

Referencing the gathering of these people that will surely one day take place, Isaiah said, "Behold, these shall come from far: and, lo, these from the north and from the west; and these from the land of Sinim" (Isaiah 49:12).

Jeremiah spoke of those who would come "from the land of the north, and from all the lands whither he hath driven them..." (Jer. 16:15). And he added that they would be hunted "...from every mountain, and from every hill, and out of the holes of the rocks" (Jer. 16:16).

Both Isaiah and Nephi make reference to this segment of Israel who will have been scattered and whose identity will have been lost among the Gentiles. As the Lord calls them forth again in preparation for the great gathering, Israel will be surprised at the number and overwhelming impact of their presence: "The children whom thou shalt have, after thou hast lost the first, shall again in thine ears say: the place is too strait for me; give place to me that I may dwell.

"Then shalt thou say in thine heart: Who hath begotten me these, seeing I have lost my children, and am desolate, a captive, and removing to and fro? And who hath brought up these? Behold, I was left alone; these, where have they been?" (1 Nephi 21:20, 21; Isaiah 49: 20, 21).

It appears that in some way unknown to us, the people of Ephraim became prominent among those who would be scattered about the earth. They would intermix with the Gentiles, as has been stated, and would in large measure become identified with them. They may, in fact, be those "Gentiles" among whom the Lord said he would restore the gospel in the last days (see 3 Nephi 16:7).

If we recall that Ephraim received the birthright blessing through his father Joseph, as pronounced by Jacob (see Genesis 48:8-20), then it should not surprise us that it would be through the seed of Ephraim that the Lord would lay the foundation for the final dispensation of the gospel upon the earth. It would account in some measure for the fact that so many of the converted members of the Church in the early part of this dispensation would be told in their patriarchal blessings that they are the seed of Joseph through Ephraim. It would help to explain the Lord's declaration to Joseph Smith in a revelation given in 1831: "Behold, the Lord requireth the heart and a willing mind: and the willing and obedient shall eat the good of the land of Zion in these last days.

"And the rebellious shall be cut off out of the land of Zion, and shall be sent away, and shall not inherit the land.

"For, verily I say that the rebellious are not of the blood of Ephraim, wherefore they shall be plucked out" (D&C 64:34-36).

It also would help to explain why the Lord would provide for those "who are in the north countries" (D&C 133:26) to come to Zion, as they are moved upon to assemble, to "fall down and be crowned with glory, even in Zion, by the hands of the servants of the Lord, even the children of Ephraim" (D&C 133:32).

The fifth and final segment of the house of Israel today are those who are of Gentile blood, who accept Jesus Christ as their Savior and his gospel as God's plan for salvation and eternal life. They receive the saving ordinances performed by proper authority. Of them the Lord has said: "...if the Gentiles will repent and return unto me, saith the

Father, behold they shall be numbered among my people, O house of Israel" (3 Nephi 16:13).

An angel of the Lord confirmed this matter with Nephi, the son of Lehi, when he said: "And it shall come to pass, that if the Gentiles shall hearken unto the Lamb of God in that day that he manifest himself unto them in word, and also in power, in very deed, unto the taking away of their stumbling blocks...

"And harden not their hearts against the Lamb of God, ...they shall be numbered among the house of Israel..." (1 Nephi 14:1, 2).

From Nephi we also receive the following: "For behold, I say unto you that as many of the Gentiles as will repent are the covenant people of the Lord; and as many of the Jews as will not repent shall be cast off..." (2 Nephi 30:2).

Abraham was told, "...for as many as receive this Gospel shall be called after thy name, and shall be accounted thy seed, and shall rise up and bless thee, as their father" (Abr. 2:10).

Those of the house of Israel today, then, fall generally into five categories.

First: The house of Judah, or the Jews.

Second: The branch of Joseph who came to the new world in 600 B.C., the Lamanites and Nephites; those with a Book of Mormon lineage.

Third: The lost tribes who appear to have remained in a somewhat coherent group, presently unidentified to us.

Fourth: Scattered remnants of the tribes of Israel who are dispersed to all parts of the earth, who have become identified with the Gentiles, and who have a generous representation of the house of Joseph.

Fifth: True Gentiles who accept the gospel of Jesus Christ and receive the ordinances of salvation and exaltation.

CHAPTER 9

The Promised Gathering and Restoration

As the prophets of the Old Testament period foresaw and foretold the downfall and scattering of Israel, they were also permitted to see and record many of the dramatic and culminating events associated with the gospel's restoration, and the fulfilling of God's promises to his covenant people. Latter-day prophets and those who kept the Book of Mormon record have shared the same vision. As the millennial reign of the Savior approaches, we must bear in mind the magnitude of the work that must be accomplished prior to and during the thousand-year period as the Lord and his servants complete all that the Father has given them to do.

The revelation that came to President Joseph F. Smith and is now incorporated in the Doctrine and Covenants as Section 138 gives us one window by which we may glimpse the extent of the effort that still lies ahead. The enormous task of taking the gospel to all of the earth's present inhabitants, as well as to those who have lived and died in all of the earlier ages without a full opportunity to learn of life's true purpose, is by itself almost beyond comprehension. When to that is added the necessity of performing essential ordinances for all who require a proxy to represent them, the vision of the work is expanded even further.

There will be the need to provide leadership in the kingdom of God upon the earth as all other kingdoms fail. It is not difficult to envision the range of responsibilities that will be carried by the Lord's agent people as they respond to their foreordained role. Ezekiel recorded these words of the Lord to him: "Son of man, when the house of Israel dwelt in their own land, they defiled it by their own way and by their doings...

"Wherefore I poured my fury upon them for the blood that they had shed upon the land, and for their idols wherewith they had polluted it.

"And I scattered them among the heathen, and they were dispersed through the countries: according to their way and according to their doings I judged them.

"And when they entered unto the heathen, whither they went, they profaned my holy name, when they said to them, These are the people of the Lord, and are gone forth out of his land.

"But I had pity for my holy name, which the house of Israel had profaned among the heathen, whither they went.

"Therefore say unto the house of Israel, Thus saith the Lord God; I do not this for your sakes, O house of Israel, but for my holy name's sake, which ye have profaned among the heathen, whither ye went.

"And I will sanctify my great name, which was profaned among the heathen, which ye have profaned in the midst of them; and the heathen shall know that I am the Lord, saith the Lord God, when I shall be sanctified in you before their eyes.

"For I will take you from among the heathen, and gather you out of all countries, and will bring you into your own land.

"Then will I sprinkle clean water upon you, and ye shall be clean: from all your filthiness, and from all your idols, will I cleanse you.

"A new heart also will I give you, and a new spirit will I put within you: and I will take away the stony heart out of your flesh, and I will give you a heart of flesh.

"And I will put my spirit within you, and cause you to walk in my statutes, and ye shall keep my judgments and do them.

"And ye shall dwell in the land that I gave to your fathers; and ye shall be my people, and I will be your God" (Ezekiel 36:17-28).

This declaration by the Lord is an excellent summary of why Israel was scattered in ancient times, as well as how the Lord will renew his covenant with them and gather them once again to their own lands. Israel will have done nothing to merit this great blessing, but the Lord will demonstrate to all people that he has the power and the integrity to fulfill his promises.

For generations, the people of Israel praised and reverenced the God "who led them out of the land of Egypt." They recognized and remembered the great miracles performed through Moses and Aaron to free them from Egyptian bondage and preserve them from the armies of Pharaoh. No events had occurred in their generations which had overshadowed these miraculous manifestations of the Lord's power in behalf of his covenant people. However, as Jeremiah looked forward to the time of Israel's ultimate restoration and envisioned the manner in which the Lord would "make bare his arm in the eyes of all nations" (see Isaiah 52:10; 3 Nephi 16-20) to redeem his people, he predicted that the events of Moses' deliverance would fade into insignificance by comparison. Jeremiah proclaimed: "Therefore, behold the days come, saith the Lord, that it shall no more be said, The Lord liveth, that brought up the children of Israel out of the land of Egypt;

"But, The Lord liveth, that brought up the children of Israel from the land of the north, and from all the lands whither he had driven them: and I will bring them again into their land that I gave unto their fathers" (Jeremiah 16:14-15).

As the Savior reviewed these forthcoming events with the branch of Israel in the new world during his brief ministry among them, he said: "Ye remember that I spake unto you, and said that when the words of Isaiah should be fulfilled – behold they are written, ye have them before you, therefore search them –

"And verily, verily, I say unto you, that when they shall be fulfilled, then is the fulfilling of the covenant which the Father hath made unto his people, O house of Israel.

"And then shall the remnants, which shall be scattered abroad upon the face of the earth, be gathered in from the east and from the west, and from the south and from the north; and they shall be brought to the knowledge of the Lord their God who hath redeemed them" (3 Nephi 20: 11-13).

"And then shall the words of Isaiah be fulfilled, which say:

"Thy watchmen shall lift up the voice; with the voice together shall they sing, for they shall see eye to eye when the Lord shall bring again Zion.

"Break forth into joy, sing together, ye waste places of Jerusalem; for the Lord hath comforted his people, he hath redeemed Jerusalem.

The Lord hath made bare his holy arm in the eyes of all the nations; and all the ends of the earth shall see the salvation of God" (3 Nephi 16:18-20).

Isaiah did, indeed, prophesy much concerning the restoration and gathering of Israel, as did Jeremiah and Amos and others of the prophets. We can learn much about future events through careful study of these prophecies.

Isaiah prophesied of the gathering: "Thus saith the Lord, in an acceptable time have I heard thee, and in a day of salvation have I helped thee; and I will preserve thee, and give thee for a covenant of the people, to establish the earth, to cause to inherit the desolate heritages;

"That thou mayest say to the prisoners, Go forth; to them that are in darkness, shew yourselves. They shall feed in the ways, and their pastures shall be in all high places.

"They shall not hunger nor thirst; neither shall the heat nor the sun smite them; for he that hath mercy on them shall lead them, even by the springs of water shall he guide them.

"And I will make my mountains a way, and my highways shall be exalted.

"Behold, these shall come from far: and, lo, these from the north and from the west; and these from the land of Sinim" (Isaiah 49:8-12).

More will be said later to add meaning to these words of Isaiah. It is perhaps well within the mark to say that some of the greatest events in the earth's mortal history are still ahead of us as the gathering of Israel continues in this last great dispensation before the Lord's triumphant return.

Joseph Smith, in speaking about the American Indians, pointed out that they are of the tribe of Joseph and that they have an inheritance here in the Americas. He said, "...And unto it (the land of America) all the tribes of Israel will come, with as many of the Gentiles as shall comply with the requisitions of the new covenant. But the tribe of Judah will return to old Jerusalem" (Teachings of the Prophet Joseph Smith, p. 17).

It will be necessary to say more later about the coming of the tribes of Israel to the land of America, but the reference to the house of Judah gathering separately to old Jerusalem is worthy of note and further comment.

In the April General Conference of the Church in 1840, Orson Hyde, one of the Twelve Apostles of the Church, received an assignment from Church leaders to undertake a mission to Jerusalem for the purpose of dedicating that land for the return of the Jews (see History of the Church, Vol. 4, p. 106). His acceptance of that assignment was in itself an act of great faith. It was not until October of 1841 that Elder Hyde was able to make his way to the Holy City. On a Sunday morning, October 21, he went to the Mount of Olives and offered his prayer of dedication. In the prayer, Elder Hyde uttered these words respecting the Jews: "Incline them to gather in upon this land according to Thy word. Let them come like clouds and like doves to their windows. Let the large ships of the nations bring them from the distant isles; and let kings become their nursing fathers, and queens, with motherly fondness, wipe the tear of sorrow from their eye" (Orson Hyde Pamphlet, Joseph S. Hyde, compiler).

Against terrible odds, and overcoming seemingly insurmountable obstacles, the Jews have begun to respond to inner promptings to return to their ancient homeland. There will yet be much travail in that part of the world. The trials faced by the people of Judah will prepare them for their ultimate acceptance of Jesus Christ as their promised Messiah.

Ezekiel, speaking for the Lord, said of that time: "Thus saith the Lord God: In that day that I shall have cleansed you from all your iniquities I will also cause you to dwell in the cities, and the waste places shall be builded.

"And the desolate land shall be tilled, whereas it lay desolate in the sight of all that passed by.

"And they shall say, This land that was desolate is become like a garden of Eden; and the waste and desolate and ruined cities are become fenced, and are inhabited...I the Lord have spoken it, and I will do it" (Ezekiel 36:33-36).

In the time of Judah's greatest extremities, they will have the Lord's promise to rely upon: "Behold, I will make Jerusalem a cup of trembling unto all the people round about, when they shall be in the siege both against Judah and against Jerusalem.

"And in that day shall I make Jerusalem a burdensome stone for all people: all that burden themselves with it shall be cut in pieces, though all the people of the earth be gathered together against it."

"In that day shall the Lord defend the inhabitants of Jerusalem; and he that is feeble among them at that day shall be as David; and the house of David shall be as God, as the angel of the Lord before them.

"And it shall come to pass in that day, that I will seek to destroy all the nations that come against Jerusalem.

"And I will pour upon the house of David, and upon the inhabitants of Jerusalem, the spirit of grace and of supplications: and they shall look upon me whom they have pierced, and they shall mourn for him, as one mourneth for his only son, and shall be in bitterness for him, as one that is in bitterness for his firstborn" (Zechariah 12:2,3, 8-10).

It is of this time that the Savior has said: "And then shall the Jews look upon me and say: What are these wounds in thine hands and in thy feet?

"Then shall they know that I am the Lord; for I will say unto them: These are the wounds with which I was wounded in the house of my friends. I am he who was lifted up. I am Jesus that was crucified. I am the son of God" (D&C 45:51-52).

Of the branch of Joseph who came to the new world and who gave us the sacred record in the Book of Mormon, much has also been prophesied. We are witnessing today the literal fulfillment of Nephi's prophecies concerning his people who would survive the terrible fratricidal conflicts of the period about 400 years after the resurrected Savior's visit among them. They would later face the ravages inflicted upon them by the Gentile nations who would come to the western hemisphere and take possession of the land. Nephi said of this time: "And it came to pass that I beheld many multitudes of Gentiles upon the land of promise; and I beheld the wrath of God, that it was upon the seed of my brethren; and they were scattered before the Gentiles and were smitten" (1 Nephi 13-14).

As Jeremiah, Isaiah, and others of the Old Testament prophets were permitted to see beyond the desolation of Israel to a time of new promise and hope, so were Nephi and other Book of Mormon prophets blessed. Nephi declared: "...in the latter days, when our seed shall have dwindled in unbelief, yea, for the space of many years, and many generations after the Messiah shall be manifested in body unto the children of men, then shall the fullness of the gospel of the Messiah come unto the Gentiles, and from the Gentiles unto the remnant of our seed–

"And at that day shall the remnant of our seed know that they are of the house of Israel, and that they are the covenant people of the Lord; and then shall they know and come to a knowledge of their forefathers, and also to the knowledge of the gospel of their Redeemer, which was ministered unto their fathers by him; wherefore, they shall come to the knowledge of their Redeemer, and the very points of his doctrine, that they may know how to come unto him and be saved" (1 Nephi 15:13-14).

It should be pointed out that, unlike the Jews who have in some measure retained the recognition of their place among the covenant people, the Nephites and the Lamanites who survived through the years lost their understanding of their true identity. It is for this reason that Nephi gives such emphasis to the importance of their coming to know that they are of the house of Israel and to a knowledge of their fathers. It is why Mormon would exclaim in his final recorded charge to them: "Know ye that ye are of the house of Israel" (Mormon 7:2). Nephi revels in the knowledge that the day will come when his people will realize who they really are: "And then at that day will they not rejoice and give praise unto their everlasting God, their rock and their salvation? Yea, at that day, will they not receive the strength and the nourishment of the true vine? Yea, will they not come unto the true fold of God?

"Behold, I say unto you, yea: they shall be remembered again among the house of Israel; they shall be grafted in, being a natural branch of the olive-tree, into the true olive tree" (1 Nephi 15:15-16).

At the time of this writing, the Church is experiencing its greatest growth among those who can trace their lineage to that small group of Josephites who came to the new world almost 2600 years ago. They too have been through times of testing and trial. Their day of promise has come but has only reached its dawning.

In 1845, the Twelve Apostles of the Church of Jesus Christ of Latter-Day Saints issued a formal proclamation to the world concerning the establishment of God's Church and Kingdom upon the earth. Referencing the remnant of Joseph in America, who had become known as the Indians, the proclamation, in a prophetic spirit, declares:

"The despised and degraded son of the forest, who has wandered in dejection and sorrow, and suffered reproach, shall then drop his disguise, and stand forth in manly dignity, and exclaim to the Gentiles who have envied and sold him: "I am Joseph: does my father yet live?" Or, in other words, I am a descendant of that Joseph who was sold into Egypt. You have hated me, and sold me, as though I was dead. But lo! I live, and am heir to the inheritance, titles, honors, priesthood, scepter, crown, throne, and eternal life and dignity of my fathers who live forevermore.

"He shall then be ordained, washed, anointed with holy oil, and arrayed in fine linen, even in the glorious and beautiful garments and royal robes of the high priesthood, which is after the order of the Son of God; and shall enter into the congregation of the Lord, even into the Holy of Holies, there to be crowned with authority and power which shall never end" (Proclamation of the Twelve Apostles of the Church of Jesus Christ of Latter-day Saints, April 6, 1845).

We have seen that prophetic declaration fulfilled, and its fulfillment will continue to reach many more of Joseph's seed in their land of promise.

The continuence of the Lord's work among the remnant of Joseph in the lands of America has significant implications for the restoration and gathering of Israel among the other segments of the covenant people.

As the Savior instructed the Nephites and Lamanites during his visit with them, he spoke of the forthcoming renewal of his covenant with Israel. To them he said: "And verily, I say unto you, I give unto you a sign, that ye may know the time when these things shall be about to take place – that I shall gather in from their long dispersion, my people, O house of Israel, and shall establish again among them my Zion.

"And when these things come to pass that thy seed shall begin to know these things – it shall be a sign unto them, that they may know that the work of the Father hath already commenced unto the fulfilling of the covenant which he hath made unto the people who are of the house of Israel.

"And then shall the work of the Father commence at that day, even when this gospel shall be preached among the remnant of this people. Verily I say unto you, at that day shall the work of the Father commence among all the dispersed of my people, yea, even the tribes which have been lost, which the Father hath led away out of Jerusalem" (3 Nephi 21:1, 7, 26).

With the Church now firmly established among those of Book of Mormon heritage, the sign spoken of by the Lord has certainly been given. This leads us to consider the lost tribes and what lies ahead for them.

As was indicated in an earlier chapter, the lost tribes, as a body, are regularly spoken of in the scriptures as being in the "north country." The Lord's reference to them in the 133rd Section of the Doctrine and Covenants seems to confirm this. It also appears that they, as was true of the Nephites and the Lamanites, have forgotten their heritage among the house of Israel. The Lord declares in this revelation: "And they who are in the north countries shall come in remembrance before the Lord..." (D&C 133:26). Something will apparently occur to bring them to a realization that they are the seed of Abraham. There will be those among them whom the Lord identifies as "prophets." These leaders will "hear his voice." They will be moved upon by the spirit to assemble in Zion; they "shall no longer stay themselves." Miraculous events will occur that will likely overshadow the exodus of Israel from Egypt in Moses' day. Hence, Jeremiah's declaration: "Therefore, behold, the days come, saith the Lord, that it shall no more be said, The Lord liveth that brought up the children of Israel from the land of Egypt;

"But, the Lord liveth, that brought up the children of Israel from the land of the north..." (Jer. 16:15-16).

The Lord speaks of a "highway that shall be cast up in the midst of the great deep" (D&C 133:27). We can only speculate on the real meaning of this phrase. Certainly it suggests that the Lord will expedite the movement of these people. Isaiah, speaking of these same events, said: "And there shall be a highway for the remnant of his people, which shall be left, from Assyria; like as it was to Israel in the day that he came up out of the land of Egypt" (Isaiah 10:16; 2 Nephi 21:16).

Isaiah adds this prophetic declaration: "Then shall the lame man leap as an hart, and the tongues of the dumb sing: for in the wilderness shall waters break out, and streams in the desert.

"And the parched ground shall become a pool, and the thirsty land springs of water: in the habitation of dragons, where each lay, shall be grass with reeds and rushes.

"And an highway shall be there, and a way, and it shall be called The way of holiness; the unclean shall not pass over it..."

"And the ransomed of the Lord shall return, and come to Zion with songs and everlasting joy upon their heads: they shall obtain joy and gladness, and sorrow and sighing shall flee away" (Isaiah 35:6-8; 10).

In his revelation to Joseph Smith, the Lord seems to confirm the words of Isaiah. As he speaks of the coming of those from the north countries to the land of Zion, he declares that "...in the barren deserts there shall come forth pools of living water; and the parched ground shall no longer be a thirsty land" (D&C 133:29).

With the coming of these people, the Lord says: "And the boundaries of the everlasting hills shall tremble at their presence" (D&C 133:31).

All of this seems to suggest that the hosts who come will be in great numbers. Even the desert areas will need to be made productive to sustain them, and they will press even against the boundaries of the land.

There is some indication in the Lord's description of these momentous events that the assembling of the lost tribes will be resisted. He declared: "Their enemies shall become a prey unto them" (D&C 133:28). As he spoke to the Nephites of these same developments, he said: "Thy hand shall be lifted up upon thine adversaries, and all thy enemies shall be cut off.

"And I will gather my people together as a man gathereth his sheaves unto the floor.

"For I will make my people with whom the Father hath covenanted, yea, I will make thy horn iron, and I will make thy hoofs brass. And thou shalt beat in pieces many people; and I will consecrate their gain unto the Lord, and their substance unto the Lord of the whole earth. And behold, I am he that doeth it" (3 Nephi 20:17-20).

As we peruse these prophetic declarations, it is not difficult to conjure up scenes reminiscent of Joshua's leading the hosts of Israel back into the land of Canaan after Israel's 400-year absence. In the interim, other people had moved into the land, had built cities, cultivated the land, planted vineyards and pastures. The Lord told Israel to take the land and all that had been developed by its most recent inhabitants.

Joseph Smith uttered these sobering words concerning the assembling of the lost tribes in the land of Zion: "And now I am prepared to say by the authority of Jesus Christ, that not many years shall pass away before the United States shall present such a scene of bloodshed as has not a parallel in the history of our nation; pestilence, hail, famine, and earthquake will sweep the wicked of this generation from off the face of the land, to open and prepare the way for the return of the lost tribes of Israel from the north country" ("Teachings of the Prophet Joseph Smith," p. 17).

This is, perhaps, why the Lord would make the following declaration to the Nephites and Lamanites when he ministered among them, referring to the period following the latter-day restoration of the gospel: "Yea, wo be unto the Gentiles except they repent; for it shall come to pass in that day, saith the Father, that I will cut off thy horses out of the midst of thee, and I will destroy thy chariots;

"And I will cut off the cities of thy land, and throw down all thy strongholds" (3 Nephi 21:14, 15).

The Lord, however, makes this reassuring promise to those who are called Gentiles in this promised land: "But if the Gentiles will repent and return unto me, saith the Father, behold they shall be numbered among my people, O house of Israel.

"And I will not suffer my people who are of the house of Israel, to go through among them, and tread them down, saith the Father" (3 Nephi 16:13, 14).

As the Savior reviewed these events with the remnant in America, he told them of Israel's restoration in the last days. "And then shall that which is written come to pass," he said; and turning directly to the words of Isaiah, he continued:

"Sing, O barren, thou that didst not travail with child..." It is obvious that the "barren" in this verse refers to Israel, who have been outcasts and unfruitful for many generations. "...for more are the children of the desolate than the children of the married wife, saith the Lord." The children of the "desolate" once again has reference to Israel, but who are the children of the "married wife"?

The scriptures often refer to the Savior as the "Bridegroom" (see D&C 33:17; Matt. 25:7); and the Church is spoken of in the same context as the "bride" (see D&C 109:73, 74; Ephes. 5:22-30). If this reference to the "married wife" could be allegorically interpreted as the Church, and the "children of the married wife" as members of the Church, the hidden meaning in this phrase becomes very significant. Does it suggest that when Israel reawakens to her true identity and stands forth in her covenant role in the fullness of times, those who have been lost and scattered and desolate will actually outnumber those who have become members of the Church in that same period? It is an interesting prospect to consider, especially in the light of the verses which follow: "Enlarge the place of thy tent, and let them stretch forth the curtains of thy habitations; spare not, lengthen thy cords and strengthen thy stakes;

"For thou shalt break forth on the right hand and on the left, and <u>thy seed shall inherit the gentiles and make the desolate cities to be inhabited</u>" (3 Nephi 22:1-3).

The beautiful verses which follow reflect the undying love the Lord feels for his covenant children, even though they have been wayward and forsaken for a time:

"Fear not, for thou shalt not be ashamed; neither be thou confounded, for thou shalt not be put to shame; for thou shalt forget the shame of thy youth, and shalt not remember the reproach of thy youth, and shalt not remember the reproach of thy widowhood any more.

"For thy Maker, thy husband, the Lord of Hosts is his name; and thy Redeemer, the Holy One of Israel—the God of the whole earth shall he be called.

"For the Lord hath called thee as a woman forsaken and grieved in spirit, and a wife of youth, when thou wast refused, saith thy God.

"For a small moment have I forsaken thee, but with great mercies will I gather thee."

"For the mountains shall depart and the hills be removed, but my kindness shall not depart from thee, neither shall the covenant of my peace be removed, saith the Lord that hath mercy on thee."

"And all thy children shall be taught of the Lord; and great shall be the peace of thy children" (3 Nephi 22:4-7, 10, 13).

Returning to the Lord's revelation of the assembling of those from the north countries (D&C 133) to the land of Zion, it is important to note several other significant points that are made. The Lord's language in this revelation is not allegorical; it is straightforward and not difficult to understand. As they come, the Lord says, "...they shall bring forth their rich treasures unto the children of Ephraim, my servants" (D&C 133:30).

Is it not possible that among those rich treasures will be their records that Nephi promised would one day come forth to take their place with the Bible and the Book of Mormon as testaments of Jesus Christ and his gospel (see 2 Nephi 29:11-14)?

"And it shall come to pass that my people, which are of the house of Israel, shall be gathered home unto the lands of their possessions; and my word also shall be gathered in one. And I will show unto them that fight against my word and against my people, who are of the house of Israel, that I am God, and that I covenanted with Abraham that I would remember his seed forever" (2 Nephi 29:14).

The tribes that have been lost will come to Zion, bringing their rich treasures to the children of Ephraim. "And there shall they fall down and be crowned with glory, even in Zion, by the hands of the servants of the Lord, even the children of Ephraim.

"And they shall be filled with songs of everlasting joy" (D&C 133:32, 33).

The role of Ephraim in these momentous events is of great interest and significance. Ephraim carries the birthright responsibility. It was among Ephraim, principally, that the foundations of the Church were laid in this last dispensation. An Ephraimite prophet, Joseph Smith, was the Lord's instrument of the restoration, and it was he who received the keys of the culminating work that would be done in this dispensation of the fullness of times. Ephraim would act as the Lord's servant in conferring the blessing of the gospel upon the heads of those of the other tribes who would "come in remembrance before the Lord" after a dark and dismal day. What could be more appropriate and more consistent with the orderliness of God's plan?

One important point remains to be made with reference to the lost tribes. While they will all come to the land of Zion to receive certain blessings at the hands of Ephraim, all but the descendants of Joseph will eventually return to their original lands of inheritance. Joseph Smith acknowledged that all but Judah would one day assemble in America. He said, referring initially to the descendants of Joseph that were brought to these lands by Lehi: "...we learn that our western tribes of Indians are descendants from that Joseph who was sold into Egypt, and that the land of America is a promised land unto them, and unto it all the tribes of Israel will come—But the tribe of Judah will return to old Jerusalem" (Teachings of the Prophet Joseph Smith, page 17).

The tribe of Judah will not assemble in America. They will return to Jerusalem to await the Savior's appearance to them. But the other tribes will assemble here, as we have explained. After they have been blessed at the hands of Ephraim, and in a time the Lord will determine, they will return to their ancient inheritances. Moroni confirms this as he makes commentary in his translation of the plates of Ether. These are his words:

"Wherefore, the remnant of the house of Joseph shall be built upon this land; and it shall be a land of their inheritance; and they shall build up a holy city unto the Lord, like unto the Jerusalem of old; and they shall no more be confounded until the end come when the earth shall pass away.

"And there shall be a new heaven and a new earth; and they shall be like unto the old save the old have passed away, and all things have become new.

"And then cometh the New Jerusalem; and blessed are they who dwell therein, for it is they whose garments are white through the blood of the lamb; and they are they who are numbered among the remnant of the seed of Joseph, who were of the house of Israel.

"And then also cometh the Jerusalem of old; and the inhabitants thereof, blessed are they, for they have been washed in the blood of the Lamb; and they are they who were scattered and gathered in from the four quarters of the earth, and from the north countries, and are partakers of the fulfilling of the covenant which God made with their father Abraham" (Ether 13:8-11).

These words of Moroni confirm that it will be more than Lehi's seed who will build up the New Jerusalem, although his righteous descendants will have part in this great work. The remnant of Jacob unto whom the Lord has given this land for their inheritance, the Gentiles who will repent and be numbered among the remnant, and "as many of the house of Israel as shall come" (3 Nephi 21:22, 23) will all participate in this wonderful project.

Reference has been made to those of Israel who would be scattered to the "four quarters of the earth," among whom the people of Ephraim would be prominent. These will also be gathered in. It is of interest, as has already been mentioned, to note how they are consistently distinguished from the main body of the lost tribes in the prophecies and scriptural references that pertain to them. They have the same promise of restoration and gathering that applies to all other segments of the house of Israel. Joseph Smith and Oliver Cowdery received from Moses in the Kirtland temple "keys of the gathering of Israel from the four parts of the earth" as well as for "the leading of the ten tribes from the land of the north" (D&C 110:11). This gathering has been taking place since the ushering in of this dispensation, and it will continue among all nations until the Lord declares that the work is finished.

CHAPTER 10
The Last Great Challenge

The story of the house of Israel continues. The last acts in this great drama have the promise of being the most exciting and stirring of all. The responsibilities that will fall upon the Lord's covenant people in these concluding scenes will be of the greatest magnitude. There are yet many testing and humbling experiences ahead for Abraham's seed, but there will be days of rejoicing as well, as the Lord fulfills every facet of his covenant, so that not one jot nor tittle is overlooked.

One important fact must be kept in mind: while it is a marvelous privilege to claim an Israelitish heritage, it is not enough simply to be of the lineage of Abraham, Isaac, and Jacob. Those of the covenant must accept Christ as their Savior and Redeemer. They must willingly align themselves with the Lord's purposes, repent of their sins, be baptized and receive the other saving ordinances. They must make and keep the individual covenants that will qualify them to be a part of the covenant group.

This is why Nephi cautioned: "For behold, I say unto you that as many of the Gentiles as shall repent are the covenant people of the Lord; and as many of the Jews (Israel) as will not repent shall be cast off" (2 Nephi 30:2).

Mormon had this concern when he recorded his final counsel to his own seed: "Know ye that ye are of the house of Israel.

"Know ye that ye must come unto repentance, or ye cannot be saved.

"Know ye that ye must lay down your weapons of war, and delight no more in the shedding of blood, and take them not again, save it be that the Lord shall command you.

"Know ye that ye must come to the knowledge of your fathers, and repent of all your sins and iniquities, and believe in Jesus Christ, that he is the Son of God..."

"And ye will also know that ye are the remnant of the seed of Jacob; therefore ye are numbered among the people of the first covenant; and if it so be that ye believe in Christ, and are baptized, first with water, then with fire and the Holy Ghost, following the example of our Savior, according to that which he hath commanded us, it shall be well with you in the day of judgment" (Mormon 7:2-5, 10).

The Savior himself would say to those who felt that their lineage alone would qualify them for the Lord's blessing: "Bring forth therefore fruits meet for repentance:

"And think not to say within yourselves, We have Abraham to our father: for I say unto you, that God is able of these stones to raise up children unto Abraham" (Matt. 3:8, 9).

The people of the covenant have not always fulfilled the Lord's expectations. They must do so now. Much is at stake, not only for themselves, but for all those who must look to God's agent people to mark the right way. This is the yoke bound upon the necks of those who have been chosen to perform a special service. It is the great privilege that the Father has extended to his most trusted children.

INDEX
People of Destiny